Hand-Me-Down Dreams

For my mother,
Kathryn Carr Jacobsen

In memory of my father and grandmother,
Cleve Robbs Jacobsen and Mary Harriet Sweeney Carr

Contents

Part Five: Looking Ahead

Acknowledgments

This book developed from a workshop on family history and careers that I first taught for Radcliffe Career Programs eight years ago. I want to thank Phyllis Stein and Ann Dart, then director and assistant director, respectively, for enabling me to offer that early version of my workshop. I would never have developed later versions of the workshop, nor this book, without that beginning.

Over the years, I have learned a tremendous amount from the people who have attended my lectures and workshops, both career professionals and the general public. I have also benefited from the advice and encouragement of friends or colleagues who read different versions of the manuscript along the way, especially Karen From, Kim Cromwell, Draper Shreve, and Christopher Bram. I'm grateful to Meme Drumwright for her help with my book proposal, and for her enthusiastic support of my workshops and my book. I owe a special debt of gratitude to Harriet Lerner, who was generous enough to read my manuscript in an early stage and offered kind words of support.

I'm grateful to my agent, Felicia Eth, for her tenacity and faith that my book would find a publishing home. And I appreciate the efforts of my editor, PJ Dempsey, to ensure that the book's style would be as accessible as possible, its ideas stated clearly and straightforwardly.

I want to thank my mother, Kathryn C. Jacobsen, my sister, Jean Jacobsen, and my brother, Kurt Jacobsen, for their love and support. Finally, I want to thank my partner, Mary C. Gentile, for her relentless faith and optimism, and her unerring knack for keeping me more logical and organized than is my natural inclination.

Introduction

In 1986, I began work on a graduate degree in social work. I was thirty-five years old, had already earned a graduate degree in English, and had started and stopped several previous careers ranging from teaching and educational administration to public relations. Finally, I felt I was on the right track. My goal was to become a psychotherapist in private practice. After two years of graduate school and two years of supervised work experience, I finally attained this goal.

Soon after beginning my work as a therapist, I visited my mother for Christmas. I sat across the kitchen table from her one morning drinking coffee, and discussed how much I enjoyed working with clients. I described my relief at finally doing work that both fascinated and fulfilled me. My mother looked me in the eye and said, "Mary, you've achieved the dream I always had for myself."

I was speechless. I felt shocked and dismayed. I quickly thought, "Don't say that. It can't be true." But just as quickly I also thought, "Well, thank God it's been said. Now I don't have to do this anymore. I can find something else to do." I also felt a wave of recognition—a feeling that I'd always known but never wanted to acknowledge this truth.

I muttered a vague reply, changed the subject, and we said nothing more about the parallels between my mother's dreams and my career. Over the following weeks, however, I couldn't stop thinking about our conversation. I felt perplexed by the intensity and diversity of my responses, and began to explore my family's impact on my career. As I did, I realized that the similarities between my mother's life and my own were striking—and obvious to anyone other than me. I also realized that I had always avoided looking at those similarities. I assumed my choices were independent of my family, and I wasn't happy to consider alternative explanations.

Peering into my family history, I looked for answers. How had my career path been influenced by my family? Why had I ignored obvious similarities between my mother's goals and my own? Why was I reluctant—even wary—to explore links between my choices and my parents' dreams? Over time, I retrieved two strands of memory that answered these questions.

First, I remembered a favorite form of fantasy play I engaged in as a child. I would spend hours imagining that I was a little hero, wandering the Swiss Alps looking for "lost souls" to save—frozen, wounded travelers who had been caught in an avalanche or lost their bearings in the endless expanse of ice and snow. I wore snowshoes, a rope wrapped around my chest, and a backpack filled with Hershey bars and oranges. A huge Saint Bernard, reminiscent of the dog in *Topper,* followed me, wearing a keg of brandy around her neck. At a discreet distance, a band of brown-hooded monks followed us with a dogsled.

I imagined the dog sniffing out the location of the lost souls. Then I would gently pour brandy over their parched, cracked lips, restoring vitality to their wounded spirits. The monks then transported the saved souls to their lodge, where they warmed them, fed them, and guided them down the mountain to safety. The grateful travelers would offer gratitude and rewards, but I never accepted them. My dog and I receded from the spotlight once our passengers were safe. I performed heroic deeds for the pride and satisfaction of knowing I had been a good girl. Good girls—heroic girls—save lives because it is their duty and honor to do so. They are embarrassed by fuss and rewards. That's the code.

As I recalled this fantasy play, I couldn't remember where the "code" came from. No one in my family ever told me it was my duty to save lives, or that goodness should provide its own reward. My mother and father were loving and responsible. My parents rewarded me for getting good grades, performing my chores, and being well mannered. They were happy when I was happy, and they never explicitly asked me for more than that—to make myself happy.

It took another memory to fit the puzzle pieces together. I was the third child in a family of four siblings, and the first daughter. My mother frequently told me when I was growing up how thrilled she had been to give birth to a daughter. She named me after her own mother, Mary Harriet Sweeney Carr, who had migrated to the United States from Ireland at the age of sixteen. My grandmother was remembered with fondness and admiration by all of her children as vibrant, warm, fun-loving, and the stable core of their family life. She had died of meningitis when my mother, the youngest of five siblings, was just eighteen.

My mother always spoke of her mother's premature loss as "devastating." The grief she experienced rearranged the foundations of her life, and I believe nothing and no one ever filled the void created by her mother's death. It wasn't that my mother never found sources of love and fulfillment, she did. She worked as a teacher and a nurse. She joined the Army Nurse Corps during World War II, where she met and married my father. She had four children of whom she claims to be proud, and she has always maintained an active intellectual and spiritual life.

Yet I remember as a child being aware of my grandmother's *absence* from our family life, even though none of the rest of us had ever known her. A photograph of my grandmother was always prominently displayed on the bureau in my parents' bedroom. Out of its soft black and white hues, my grandmother gazed like a foreigner from another era, her hair pulled back, rimless round glasses framing reflective eyes, her expression a half-smile suggesting rueful sadness more than mirth. As a child, I could not fathom the grief and vulnerability at the center of my mother's life that this photo represented. It contrasted with my own perceptions of my mother—strong, authoritative, utterly reliable.

Somehow I intuited as a child a fundamental vein of sadness and disappointment in my mother. I thought it was because of me—that I had failed to be the daughter my mother wanted. I was defiant and moody rather than pliant and sweet. A tomboy, I favored pants and sneakers rather than the ruffled dresses favored by my mother. From an early age, we struggled with matching intensity over how I should dress and behave. As a teenager and young adult, we argued—sometimes bitterly—about religion and politics.

Only recently have I come to understand the thwarted dream

that nourished our conflict. It began with my name, as dreams often do. I carried my grandmother's name from before my birth. A dream, nurtured for years, perhaps never consciously expressed, entered the world at the same time I did. A dream of reunion. A dream of finding what has been lost and never again regained. A dream of intimacy and happiness. As is stated in the title of Delmore Schwartz's famous short story, "in dreams begin responsibilities," and in the dream that accompanied my christening began my own responsibilities.

As children do, I instinctively understood my responsibilities. And as children do, I took them seriously, even though they were impossible responsibilities stemming from tragic, impossible dreams. Looking backward, it was easy to see the early expression of my responsibility for "saving lost souls" as I cast myself as hero in my fantasy play. In fantasy, I could succeed in a heroism I felt called upon to perform in real life but failed at.

It was painful to realize that the "lost soul" I had felt profoundly obliged to "save" was my own mother. Because I couldn't. Never could. Never would. No one *except* my mother herself ever could. But much as I understand the impossibility of the task I set for myself, my grief over that insufficiency has shaped my life as much as my mother's loss of my grandmother shaped hers. Painful as these insights have been, they have also liberated me. I have retired from the job of hero. I am no longer tempted to "save" clients' lives—I try to help them save their own. And through this book, I hope to pass on the knowledge I have gained by "retiring" from unrealistic family expectations.

My intuitive grasp of my first responsibility, the one I was assigned before birth, has given my life its deepest sense of purpose. But until I understood it, it also engendered my deepest sense of failure and frustration. This duality characterizes our families' influence on our career paths. We inherit the losses, hopes, and dreams of previous generations, and we are, like molten iron, shaped on the anvil of these experiences. They give us texture, shape, goals, and purpose. Yet if the goals are impossible, the dreams merely *hand-me-down* fulfillments for *someone else,* we will—hard as we work, loyal as we feel—never find our own happiness. We will hand down our own unfulfilled dreams to the next generation, whether we want to or not.

The language families use to communicate dreams and expectations is intuitive and paradoxical. Words do not always signify true intentions. Subtleties of body language, nuances of tone, suppressed emotions betrayed by the slightest of gestures transmit the truth of what makes parents happy or sad to the deepest layers of children's minds. Often, this truth contradicts what parents consciously would either *want* or *allow* themselves to ask of their children if they were aware of doing so. The nature of this communication, its complexity and power, is the subject of this book.

Such understanding benefits us in several ways. We can decode the messages our families have telegraphed us about whom we should become. We can redefine our responsibilities to our families in more realistic, fair, and balanced ways. We can rediscover our own hidden potentials and dreams. We can heal long-standing resentments and betrayals. And we can replace confusion and irritation with understanding and compassion.

Because I believe that much happiness derives from finding meaningful work that expresses our unique creative selves—and that great misery derives from its lack—this book concentrates on the ways our families influence our careers. Specifically, I focus on the barriers families may wittingly or unwittingly construct on our path toward satisfying work lives.

Many families support our strivings for individual happiness most of the time. Even more families support us some of the time. And even the most difficult families provide *some* support. But it is the *barriers* our family histories confront us with that cry out for attention and change. Such barriers challenge us to evolve new strategies for happiness to replace the worn-out, failed ones previous generations relied on, and have handed down to us.

In order to demonstrate how families communicate *hand-me-down dreams,* in this book I will describe individuals whose careers have been profoundly influenced by their families. These individuals are not real people, but realistic composites I have drawn from many different sources.

Traditional Native American wisdom advises us to look seven generations into the future to assess the impact of current actions. The wisdom of family systems theory advises us to look at past generations in order to fathom the deepest meaning of the present. While we may not have information about our ancestors as far back as seven generations, we can infer the ghostly imprint of these ancestors in the outlines of our parents' and grandparents' lives. For they, just as we, have inherited *their* parents' history of immigration, illness, hope, birth, catastrophe, and renewal. We have been delivered to the present by this past, and while the weight of it may seem daunting, our power to heal is not only real but enormous.

All of these generations, after all, have conspired to evolve into *us.* And by making conscious decisions about who we shall be and become, we mold our own destiny, we influence the future, and we give birth to new meanings for the past. It is important work, requiring courage, tenacity, and effort. But it's worth it. I hope this book will aid you in finding your true path.

How to Use This Book

This book is written to be read from beginning to end. It is divided into five parts, each of which builds upon information presented in the preceding chapters.

PART ONE: HAND-ME-DOWN DREAMS

The chapters in **Part One** define what hand-me-down dreams are, describe how they're passed on cyclically in all families, and illustrate how and why career-related problems arise in some. You will learn when and how you can benefit from understanding your family's past, and what makes trying to live out someone else's dream such a common and tempting but ultimately frustrating endeavor.

PART TWO: FAMILY DYNAMICS

Part Two begins by explaining generally how family members are connected emotionally as a system, then moves on to specific topics, such as the influence of sibling order and gender on family "job assignments"; "triangles" among family members and their impact on career selection; and what happens when adults rebel against or cut off their parents. These chapters enable you to correlate career problems or obstacles with the specific family dynamics described. They also offer advice on how to solve these problems.

If you're a survivor of childhood abuse, you'll find a chapter describing its impact on career and job choice. If you grew up in a family that didn't "fit in" because of race, class, or other types of social difference, there's a chapter describing the impact this experience may have had on your career dreams.

PART THREE: WORK, SUCCESS, AND MONEY

Family dynamics show up constantly in the workplace, and **Part Three** illustrates how your family's values and beliefs regarding the purpose of work, the meaning of success, and the importance of money contribute to career problems when they constrict your goals or block you from taking risks and coping with change. You will learn how replaying family "rules" about authority, teamwork, and leadership can limit your effectiveness in resolving conflicts or collaborating constructively on the job. You'll also find suggestions on how to let go of values and rules that limit you, and replace them with ones that expand your choices.

PART FOUR: LIVING YOUR OWN DREAM—7 STEPS TO RECLAIM YOUR CAREER

The chapters in **Part Four** function as a workbook, enabling you to apply the general knowledge you've gained about family influences on careers to your unique family background and your individual career path. The steps are designed to systematically take you through your family's work history and its impact on your career choice and your roles and relationships at work; assess your individual talents, interests, and passions; clarify your goals for the future; and develop a flexible but structured plan for achieving them.

PART FIVE: LOOKING AHEAD

Part Five invites you to look ahead, both to the future of your career and, for parents, to that of your children's careers. If you're a parent or expect to be, **chapter 21** explains why helping your children to follow their own dreams means preparing yourself as best you can to fulfill your own dreams. The last chapter summarizes workplace trends such as a shift from long-term jobs to short-term, contract-based employment, and discusses the importance of shifting to a view of yourself as "self-employed."

APPENDIXES

Appendix 1 offers advice on how and when to seek professional support. **Appendix 2** recommends additional reading on career development, family relationships, and workplace trends.

Part One

Hand-Me-Down Dreams

✦

1

What Are Hand-Me-Down Dreams?

Do you remember inheriting a hand-me-down sweater from an older sibling? It may have fit, but it was probably a little snug or maybe a bit too loose. It may have been green, but your favorite color was blue. It may have been a wool cardigan, but all the other kids your age were wearing cotton crewnecks. You could wear it. It kept you warm. But it wasn't something *you* would have chosen.

We all inherit dreams, goals, values, and beliefs from our families. These *hand-me-down dreams* influence every aspect of our lives, including the work we do and how we do it. As with hand-me-down garments, we may be able to "wear" these dreams, but if they aren't our own choice, they won't make us happy. They can't—they belong to someone else.

When we've inherited clothes that don't fit, the reason for our discomfort is as obvious as a split seam or a sagging hemline. But when our jobs are unfulfilling, relationships at work have soured, or our efforts to change careers are blocked by confusion and self-doubt, it may not occur to us at first to look *backward*—to explore how family history shaped our career goals.

Instead, we may look inward to inventory the peaks and valleys of our individual work history. We may look outward to the marketplace to discover which growth industries offer viable careers. These inquiries can yield important and useful strategies for career development. But if you've tried them and you *still* feel stuck, frustrated, or confused, it's time to shift your gaze homeward. To the home you grew up in. To the family members who raised you.

WHY SHOULD YOU EXPLORE YOUR FAMILY'S PAST?

Do you ever feel it's hard to think straight, stay calm, or speak honestly around your family? Or to feel as comfortable, respected, and accepted as you do with partners, colleagues, or friends? If so, you're like the vast majority of people for whom family presents a mixed bag. We love our families. We derive strength, support, and guidance from them. But at times, we experience conflict, hurt, and frustration with them, too.

The tension we feel with our families is like the tip of an iceberg—covering enduring vulnerabilities buried beneath the surface. The depths of the iceberg reveal the places inside where we depend upon our families for acceptance, approval, and esteem—or permission to live our own lives. They reveal, in short, the places inside where, regardless of age, we have not finished growing up.

It's tempting to believe that careers develop separately from family influences, that work provides a firewall against vulnerabilities. But I have never known anyone for whom this was true. You bring all of yourself to work, the awkward and unfinished parts as well as those that are confident, composed, and mature. You'll succeed beautifully when your skills, motivation, and maturity are matched with the challenges you'll encounter.

You encounter problems when one of your vulnerable, unfinished "edges" bumps up against a challenge that exposes the rawness inside. For example:

You're unhappy with your job and know you need to change careers, but you feel paralyzed and indecisive at the prospect of starting over.

You're assigned to work with a team, but you're possessive of your ideas and fearful that colleagues will steal credit for your contributions.

You have to supervise a co-worker who is older than you and are unable to delegate tasks to someone who looks like your father.

Your new boss makes unreasonable demands, but you're afraid that if you speak out on your own behalf, you'll be accused of whining.

If you lose your composure, your clarity, and your usual problem-solving ability, then chances are that your current dilemma has unmasked a layer of "iceberg" connected to your family's past. With tenacious problems like these, if you hunt for the usual suspects—unfair bosses, unreasonable tasks, unwelcome trends within your profession, anything other than *you*—you won't find the answers you need. Seeking the answers you need will take you to the only place where you can discover the unfinished places within. That place is your family's past.

WHAT YOU CAN LEARN FROM HAND-ME-DOWN DREAMS

Exploring your family's hand-me-down dreams is like rummaging through an old trunk of garments stored in the attic. You'll find answers to many questions:

- **First,** what garments do you find? What did your family expect you to wear? *In other words, which goals, interests, and behaviors did your family encourage?*
- **Second,** what garments are missing? What did you want to wear but weren't allowed to? *In other words, which goals, interests, and behaviors did your family discourage, ignore, or punish?*
- **Third,** where did your family shop? Did they buy cheap or expensive items? Plain or fancy? Did they shop carefully or impulsively? *In other words, what are your family's values about work, money, success, and happiness?*
- **Fourth,** which family members got to wear different items? Who wore tuxedos or ball gowns, who wore work shirts and blue jeans? Who wore new clothes, who wore the same old rags year after year? *In other words, what roles and rules applied to different family members?*

With this information, you can determine whether unhappiness or confusion you've experienced in your career stems from trying to force-fit yourself into a "wardrobe" that you never liked or felt comfortable with in the first place.

WHO BENEFITS FROM EXPLORING HAND-ME-DOWN DREAMS?

Everyone has a career of some kind. And everyone has a family. This book describes the intersection between these two universally shared experiences. It can, therefore, benefit almost everyone at any stage of career development. For example:

Stages of Career Development

• **Beginners.** If you're deciding on a college major or graduate program or hunting for a first job, this book can help you to determine whether you're choosing a path because it will make *you* happy or because it will make your family happy.

• **First-time managers or team leaders.** We first learn about authority, leadership, and teamwork from our families. Understanding what your family taught you about power, motivation, and rewards enables you to understand your style of leadership and to identify vulnerabilities and strengths.

• **Midlife or midcareer changers.** If you're making "course corrections" in your career path—either voluntarily or because you've been laid off—assessing your family's influence helps you to understand past career choices and equips you to make wise decisions in the future.

• **Post-retirement planners.** Retirement is becoming not the end of work, but a transition into a new stage of voluntary work that brings wholeness and balance to later years. Folding your personal work history within the larger context of your family's past can help you identify goals that will give your worklife a sense of purpose and closure.

Career Problems

Family influences can be the hidden source of a wide range of career problems. If you answer yes to *any* of these questions, learning to explore your family history through the lessons in this book will provide new ways to diagnose and solve the problem.

- Do you feel stuck in a job you dislike?
- Is your career stagnating?
- Do you encounter chronic conflict with bosses, peers, or people you supervise?

- Do you feel confused or hopeless about finding the "right" career?
- Do you know what career you want to pursue, but feel unmotivated or fearful of change?
- Have you consulted career books, counselors, interest inventories, and other resources, but still feel confused about your goals?
- Do you get taken advantage of by bosses or colleagues and want to learn why and what to do?
- Do you feel you haven't had a career, just a series of jobs?
- Do you believe you are working at less than your full potential?
- Do you feel trapped by your responsibilities and resigned to not really "living" until you retire?
- Are you afraid you're repeating your parents' lives without intending or wanting to?
- Do you find yourself taking care of people at work just as you do at home?
- Do you want to ensure that your child follows his or her own career path, rather than echoing yours?

The remaining chapters and exercises in this book will enable you to identify whether and how family influences created or sustain your problem; clarify "mismatches" between your own values and goals and those of your family; and map a career path uniquely suited to your *own* gifts and dreams.

2

The Cycle of Hand-Me-Down Dreams

The first and most helpful discovery you're likely to make as you search your family's past for solutions to current problems is this: *You are not the first in your family to experience the problem.* Just as you can trace a family heirloom back through generations of earlier owners, you can trace hand-me-down dreams back through your parents and grandparents. Most parents would never deliberately interfere with their children's ability to choose a fulfilling career. But if they haven't understood the influence of family legacies in their own lives, they will automatically pass them on to the next generation.

TO BREAK THE CYCLE, DISCOVER HOW IT STARTS

You can't break a cycle until you understand you're caught up in one. And you can't determine the patterns you're repeating—the hand-me-down dreams you've inherited—until you've explored *what* your family asked you to do, and *how* the request was communicated. For most of us, the cycle starts with the dreams and expectations communicated to us by our parents and grandparents, or whoever filled those roles in our lives regardless of biological or legal ties.

Families make requests through *direct* and *indirect* means, although some rely more on one strategy than the other. As you'll see, however, even when requests are made directly, they remain disguised *as* requests to family members, no matter how obvious they seem to outsiders. The *hidden* nature of the asking keeps the cycle strong.

DUTY, GENES, AND DESTINY: HOW DIRECT REQUESTS ARE DISGUISED

Some parents come right out and say, "Be a lawyer or a scientist because *I* need you to make me happy." But most parents don't express their expectations in such bluntly personal terms. Instead, they view their dreams for their children as gifts and opportunities that eluded their grasp, or that of previous generations. They believe their children's purpose and privilege is to take advantage of these opportunities. They tend, therefore, to describe expectations in terms of family *duty, genes,* or *destiny.*

It's Your Duty

Your parents may have emphasized your *duty* to excel in particular areas. A duty differs from a request. Duties are obligations, not invitations or favors. You can say no to a request without shame or blame. But when parents say, "Do your duty," they mean they *have the right to expect* a particular action or achievement. If you don't comply, you encounter anger or indignation. You haven't merely declined an invitation, you have reneged on an obligation.

The problem isn't the concept of duty itself. Parents fulfill their duty when they teach children the importance of honesty, nonviolence, respect, and trying hard. These are general principles of human behavior. We owe it to ourselves, our parents, and the world to fulfill these duties. Problems arise when parents distort the meaning of duty in order to disguise an *emotional need* as a *moral command.* For example, how often did you hear comments such as these when you were a child?

"No child of mine is going to get a B in math! The Spencers always get A's, and you will not be the first to lower our standards."

"I haven't spent a fortune on a private school so you could waste your time studying art history. You're going to be pre-med."

"You will not quit basketball—I didn't drive you to practice year after year so you could miss your chance at a sports scholarship."

"Major in something practical—if a business degree was good enough for your father and mother, then it's good enough for you."

If you heard such comments, you learned that grades mattered more than what you learned or the pleasure you took in learning. You learned that curiosity, creativity, and joy were less important than "practicality." You learned that being a loyal, good child meant adopting the academic subjects and extracurricular activities—and as adults, the job titles and salaries—that your parents believed you owed it to them to choose.

What Duties Are—and Aren't

Let's be clear. These lessons aren't about *duties.* They don't define general principles of human behavior. In fact, they're a recipe for unhappiness because they substitute your parents' goals for your own. They *do* define what your parents needed from you—either to boost their self-esteem or to feel compensated for the work and money they invested in your future.

Let's also be fair. Your parents probably didn't think they were manipulating you by disguising their *needs* as your *duty.* It may never have occurred to them to distinguish between the two. They were asking you for exactly what they said: your duty—just as your grandparents no doubt asked of them when they were growing up. They probably believed that complying with your grandparents' wishes meant showing the respect parents are due for raising children. They'll expect the same "respect" from you.

As a consequence of these lessons, you may have given up activities or goals that your parents viewed as unimportant, risky, or demeaning. Yet you may never have thought you were sacrificing anything. After all, you weren't *asked* to give anything up. You were never thanked for doing so. You were simply doing what was expected. What was "right." What your parents believed they were "entitled" to expect from dutiful children. What your grandparents had expected from *them.*

Three Reasons Why We Resist Connecting Childhood Duties with Our Career Choices

Most of us translate the definition of duty we learn as children into our criteria for becoming responsible adults. We apply these measures when choosing college majors, graduate programs, jobs, and employers. Yet we may resist connecting childhood duties with our career choices for these three reasons:

- **First,** we prefer to see ourselves as self-reliant.
- **Second,** we don't want to show disrespect for our parents by exposing the emotional needs beneath their definition of duty.
- **Third,** we may already have gotten good jobs, earned money, and made our parents proud—and we don't want to cause "trouble."

These are persuasive reasons. Nonetheless, you can't let them stop you from exploring differences between your duty to your parents and your duty to yourself. Ignoring the truth never made anyone self-reliant. The greatest respect you can pay your parents is telling the truth, not protecting them from it. And in the long run, more trouble is caused by ignoring the truth than by confronting it.

What Is Your Duty to Yourself?

You have to determine whether your parents' vision of what is right is truly right for you. If it isn't, you won't be happy in your work no matter how "good" your job is, how much money you make, how "practical" your decisions have been—or how good your parents feel about your career.

The following are your duties to yourself. No one is entitled to demand that you give them up—not even your parents. It's challenging to fulfill these duties at any age, but it's also both possible and necessary. What's impossible is to build a satisfying career based on anything else.

- Determine what you *want,* not what others *expect* from you.
- Define duty and practicality in your own terms, and make decisions and plans accordingly.

It's in Your Genes

Some parents describe genes as the primary influence on a child's talents and future career. The following comments suggest that children are genetically predisposed to select particular careers.

"He's a chip off the old block. He loves to play with tools. He'll be a carpenter like his dad."

"She's got her mother's flair for language. I bet she'll be a writer."

"She inherited her father's love of argument—she'll be the next lawyer in the family."

"He loves to play with Tinker Toys just like his father—he was born to be an engineer."

Such observations of predictable and repetitive traits and roles give a family coherence and a sense of distinctive, inherited identity. The problem, however, with being perceived as "like" other family members is twofold. First, you attract not just the comparison but the emotions and expectations—positive and negative—that attach to your relative. These expectations act as a prescription for how you should behave and how you will be perceived within the family.

Your family—and you, too—may not think these comparisons exert pressure on you; they simply *describe* you. Even flagrant lobbying, such as "She's such a little caretaker, she's bound to become a nurse like her mother," can remain hidden as pressure to both parent and child. In everyday speech, we may refer to someone as a "born" engineer, a "born" lawyer, or a "born" entrepreneur, but no one is born to any of these social roles. An inherited trait or a talent does not determine its uses. *You* do. But if you perceive yourself as born to a certain occupation, you won't feel free to choose. That lack of choice is the second problem that stems from being perceived as "like" your relatives: being seen as "like" someone else is different from being seen as yourself.

EMBRACE YOUR UNIQUENESS

You are unique, whether or not your family believes this is true or is happy about it. If you didn't choose your career but let your "genes"—and your family's need for continuity—choose for you, you have to clarify whether you are happy with the life your "genes" picked. If you are, you will benefit from clarifying that it's *your* choice, too. If you aren't happy, you need to embrace and define your uniqueness. Your family will have to do so as well.

To find that uniqueness, you have to stop basing your choices on being "like" anyone else, and instead base them on being true to yourself. Self-definition is challenging for everyone, but the good news is that your uniqueness is real. Just because you haven't paid attention to it doesn't mean it doesn't exist. It always has. It's only waiting for you to explore.

For help in clarifying the influence of family "genes" on your career choices, see **Exercise 15-1.** For help defining what is unique about you, see **Exercise 17-1.**

It's Your Destiny

Some families believe destiny, fate, or divine providence determines each generation's careers. Did you hear comments such as these when you were growing up?

"We're a hard-luck lot, we Pileckis never get ahead. Fate has it in for us."

"Every generation of McCoys has at least one priest. This time, God has chosen Danny."

"It's her fate to take over the family business."

"He's destined to build a fortune and save the family honor."

Whether the source of destiny is understood to be God, the stars, good or bad luck, social and economic oppression, or a combination of these, the effect of such comments on children is similar to those described regarding genes. An overruling force—this time history or bad luck rather than biology—makes the child's choice irrelevant or unnecessary. The family's emotional needs are disguised as *prophecy.*

Destiny Is Your Inner Calling

If you were brought up to believe that destiny chose your career, your challenge later in life will be to redefine destiny and reclaim the freedom to choose your work. Destiny doesn't mean that your life is predetermined by an external force. It means discovering what you feel "called" to do from within—because there are talents you need to express, purposes you want to fulfill. Anything short of that isn't destiny; it's manipulation. You have the right to discover the former, and to refuse to submit to the latter.

For help in clarifying your inner calling, see **Exercise 17-1.**

HOW INDIRECT REQUESTS ARE COMMUNICATED

Indirect requests are communicated through body language or tone of voice. Frequently these nonverbal signals contradict what we actually say. It's hard for our bodies to lie—or even to tell a partial truth. Whatever has been held back, underemphasized, or denied creeps into our tone of voice, the stiffening of our backs, a slightly arched eyebrow, or a sagging posture. Everyone exchanges this type of nonverbal message. Families usually rely upon indirect communication for requests that would, if spoken aloud, be considered rude, wrong, or selfish.

What Children Learn from Indirect Communication

Adults often believe that children see and hear only what they have been directly told to see and hear. They think, for example, that if you tell children you are calm—even though you feel worried and anxious—they will believe you. Children won't notice the quaver in your voice or the sweat on your brow; they will relax and feel secure *because you said everything was fine.* This isn't true. Children will see that you are upset, but will also understand you don't want to admit or discuss it. They will not believe that everything is fine. They may, however, conclude that there is something wrong with discussing emotions, and that it is acceptable to deny them.

It isn't that adults think children are stupid. Nor that adults themselves are stupid. Rather, adults *underestimate* children's intuitive abilities and *overestimate* their own self-knowledge and self-control. These miscalculations reflect their earlier experience growing up around adults who treated them as though their feelings and perceptions could be controlled, denied, or ignored. Under such tutelage, we stop knowing what we are feeling, when we are feeling it, and how to express our emotions.

The Paradox of "Hidden" Meanings That Everyone Detects

A paradoxical situation develops in many families. Members are finely tuned to detect the anxiety, fear, hope, or dread expressed indirectly by others. Yet members pretend or genuinely believe these nonverbal cues either don't exist or shouldn't count. Family members disclaim "hidden" meanings. And indeed, if they didn't actually say they felt unhappy or angry out loud but simply "looked" or "sounded" as if they were, who can be sure what they actually felt? Implied meanings, like beauty, are in the mind of the beholder. And therein lies the problem.

WHY INDIRECT COMMUNICATION CREATES CONFUSION

What can't be discussed cannot be clarified, disagreed with, disowned, resolved, or affirmed. Not directly, anyway. Like dominos falling in a line, indirect messages beget indirect responses. For this reason, indirect communication creates massive confusion.

At a family gathering, for example, you witness your uncle glaring at your aunt. Your aunt abruptly leaves the room. Their son slams his fist into a wall. Then their daughter begins to cry. None of them have spoken, so no one knows for sure what these individuals are feeling or why. But the room is abuzz with speculation. Everyone has a theory, but nobody knows the full truth.

Over time—in the absence of open discussion—theories substitute for truth, even though they may contradict one another. As in the Japanese film *Rashomon,* which narrates the same event from three points of view, family members will believe in multiple, sometimes starkly different "truths" about the same events. Under such circumstances, conflicts and confusion easily arise. Family members don't know whom to believe, or whether to believe what people literally say—or what their tone and gestures imply. If your family relied on indirect communication, it may take years for you to discover which of your goals were based on:

- What your parents *actually* said
- What your parents *implied* but didn't say
- What other family members said your parents *meant*
- What you yourself really wanted

Parents Send Mixed Messages Even When They're Trying Not To

Even parents who believe children should be free to develop their own budding talents and goals sometimes indirectly contradict this stance. Typically, they say directly, "Follow your own dreams. Whatever makes you happy will make us proud." They would never deliberately ask children to forsake their own dreams on their behalf. Yet on the inside, they prefer certain careers for their children. These preferences sneak into their body language, gestures, and tone of voice and undercut their direct encouragement of free choice by sending mixed messages. These nonverbal signals influence choices subtly but powerfully, because the parents' influence remains silent and invisible to both parent and child.

Sean, age fourteen, discovers that when he hits a home run during a baseball game, his father beams with pride and spontaneously hugs him. When he shows his father the A he got on his math test, his father says, "That's wonderful, son, I'm proud of you," but doesn't bother to put down the newspaper or to touch him. The disparity in his father's behavior tells Sean that schoolwork is less important than sports.

In high school, Sean's grades slip but he makes the all-star baseball team. His father rebukes Sean for letting his grades tumble, but he hugs him harder than ever when Sean wins Most Valuable Player in the all-star game. Sean continues to excel in sports but his academic performance declines. Both father and son view Sean's lack of intellectual ambition as entirely the boy's own fault.

Molly loves playing the violin. Up until the age of twelve, her parents enjoyed her practicing. But after her music teacher suggests that Molly should become a concert violinist, she finds that when she plays, her father turns the radio up loud and her mother bangs pots and pans in the kitchen. She asks if something is wrong, but her parents insist that Molly continue practicing. Molly assumes she must play badly, even though her parents assure her she's "terrific."

As Molly loses confidence in her talent, she also loses interest in playing the violin. When she asks her parents if she can quit, they say the decision is entirely up to her. When she does quit, she believes she has neither musical ability nor discipline. In high school, Molly decides to become a doctor—her father's unfulfilled ambition that had been derailed by the financial demands of an early marriage and Molly's own birth. Her parents are thrilled with her choice, especially since "it was her own idea." Later, when Molly drops out of medical school, she concludes she is truly a "quitter," incapable of commitment to any career.

UNSPOKEN REQUESTS LOSE POWER WHEN YOU "HEAR" THEM

Whenever we receive conflicting spoken and unspoken messages, the unspoken ones will command more attention and exert greater force. Indirectness conveys importance and urgency, as hidden and secret truths always do. Like the door that says DO NOT ENTER, secrecy grabs our attention and won't let go. Unspoken requests gain power because they cannot be disputed, and because they aren't supposed to be "real" or "count." Indirect requests simply burrow into our psyches and stay there until we ferret them out. The good news is that you can backtrack and clarify choices that weren't made freely but in response to unspoken emotional cues. Once you can "hear" what your parents requested, you can decide whether to say yes or no.

For help deciphering indirect requests in your family, see **Exercise 15-1.** See **chapter 4** for more on how families communicate emotions.

WHAT IF YOUR PARENTS DIDN'T CARE WHAT YOU DID?

At my Hand-Me-Down Dreams workshops someone usually asks, "What if you didn't get direct or indirect requests from your parents? My parents didn't care what I did." Since I believe no request is a kind of request, I'll ask the person to describe specifically how his or her parents responded to schoolwork and play. People usually reply that their parents seemed bored, indifferent, or too busy to pay attention. These silent behaviors speak loudly to children, presenting them with a powerful indirect request.

Rarely would a parent directly ask a child not to have any interests, not to care about school, not to get too excited about life, or not to be creative or have fun. Similarly, few would ask that a child live primarily through fantasy or daydreams, stay dependent forever, and never leave home. In effect, however, the "no requests" described above indirectly ask for these outcomes.

The Impact of Parents' Lack of Attention

Children crave and thrive on their parents' attention. When they encounter a mysterious void instead of praise, admiration, affection, warnings, or anger, they feel alone, cut off from their most important source of safety and love. If your parents were depressed, overwhelmed, numb, or always seemed bored or distracted, their behavior told you eloquently, "You're on your own." It sounds like freedom, but it isn't. It's isolating, empty, and scary. It's like floating adrift in empty space, with no inner or outer directional markers to grip on or push against.

Did your parents seem calmest and most at ease when you were quiet, introspective, lost in fantasy play or daydreams? In other words, when you were *not* making demands for their time and attention? If so, you may have learned to *shut out* the external world and to *shut down* your exuberance and curiosity. In childhood, these strategies make it easier to be quiet and unobtrusive, and thereby minimize stress on your parents. But if they become habitual, you may find it hard later in life to define tangible interests, set specific goals, and forge an independent career. In addition to confusion about your goals, the result can be prolonged financial and emotional dependence on your parents.

Why "No Requests" Presents the Hardest Challenge

"No requests," in short, asks children to perform the most challenging work of all—soothing their parents' fractured, overstressed lives. The work is hard, never finished, doesn't pay anything, and offers no chance for advancement. You won't accumulate transferable job skills, and you can't list it on your résumé. Nonetheless, never assume, as many people from such backgrounds do, that your struggle to build a career outside your family stems from laziness or emptiness.

You've never had the chance to be lazy. To the contrary, you've been working hard at taking care of your parents all your life. As with the other types of direct and indirect communication described above, just because your parents' request was masked as indifference doesn't mean you didn't understand precisely what they needed from you. You may feel empty, but *feeling* empty is not the same as *being* empty. No one is empty. But you will gradually have to learn to turn back on the ideas and energy you shut down long ago. It's hard work; it takes time; but it's possible. Getting your life back will be your reward.

See **Exercise 17-1** for assistance in discovering your goals.

WHAT YOU NEED TO FIND OUT TO MOVE BEYOND THE CYCLE

The cycle of hand-me-down dreams depends upon generational sleights of hand that disguise parents' requests as duty, destiny, genes, or—the most powerful disguise of all—*silence.* To see through the veil of these disguises, you need to find out what your parents wanted. Here's the secret: People rarely ask from others what they can easily do or have already done for themselves. The most important question you can ask, therefore, isn't "What did my parents do?" it's "What did they never get the chance to do—but wished they could or thought they should?"

Every family has stories of misadventure, missed opportunity, youthful folly, inequity, and heartbreak. These are the emotional hearths within which hand-me-down dreams are forged. Do you know the answers your parents would give to these questions?

Did the education they wanted elude them?

Was the career they aimed for not available to someone of their gender, class, or racial/ethnic background?

Did illness, accident, or poverty interfere with their career plans?

Did they follow their parents' or society's advice instead of their hearts' desires?

You may have to dig for the answers because your parents may find these stories painful to discuss or may mistakenly think you're better off not knowing. They may believe their lives before your birth had no effect on you. They may not understand that the *less* they tell you about their lives, the *greater* their influence is likely to be. Nonetheless, whatever they dreamed of but never attained, lost but never mourned, will profoundly influence your life. The fact that your parents don't understand the influence does nothing to diminish its clout. Ultimately, what matters isn't what your parents understand, it's what *you* understand, and what you do with that knowledge to improve your life.

3

The Impact of Living Someone Else's Dream

No one can fulfill someone else's dreams. It doesn't matter how much you love a person or how hard you try. The harsh but liberating truth is that it cannot be done. The only person who can fulfill a dream is the person who gave birth to it in the first place.

You can't give your parents back lost opportunities. You can't grieve their losses. You *can* be a compassionate witness to their hopes and disappointments. That is no small gift; indeed, it is among the greatest gifts anyone can offer. But it is completely different from trying to fulfill your parents' lost dreams by giving up your own. If you try to live someone else's dream, not only do you risk making yourself miserable, but you probably won't get the response you hoped for. Instead of joy and gratitude, you may encounter the opposite.

HOW PARENTS RESPOND WHEN CHILDREN LIVE OUT THEIR DREAMS

If you chose your college major, your graduate degree, or your career because it was your parents' dream, you probably expected praise, rewards, and a long vacation from further demands. Indeed, your parents may have expressed gratitude and pleasure. But did you also receive dubious, double-edged, dissatisfied "compliments" such as the following?

"I hope you don't think you can rest on your laurels just because you passed the bar."

"Don't think you're too good for your family now that you've got a college degree."

"I see your roommate graduated summa cum laude rather than magna cum laude like you. But we're still very proud of you."

"I hope you're not going to settle for vice president when you could be CEO someday."

"We're so proud you were promoted to program director. Did you hear your cousin Betty is pregnant?"

"It's a lovely book. I just didn't understand a word."

"A Ph.D. is a wonderful achievement, but isn't it time you learned something practical you could use to make a decent living?"

If your parents respond to your successes in these undercutting, devaluing ways, you probably feel angry, puzzled, betrayed, and hurt. Why do they make such deflating comments?

Are Your Parents Trying to Hurt You?

No. Probably not. Parents say hurtful, insensitive things because they don't yet understand that *you cannot fulfill their dreams.* They may not even understand that that's what they've been asking you to do. When, however, you achieve the education, the profession, or the wealth that eluded them, your success reminds them of what they never did and never will attain—except vicariously through you. It drives home the permanence of lost opportunities and sacrifices. Your parents' disappointment, frustration, envy, or sense of failure arises most intensely at your moments of greatest glory. These emotions interfere with their ability to celebrate your achievements, because their pride and joy for you are clouded with sadness for themselves.

Envy and Sorrow Bubble Up and Trickle Out as Criticism

Most people feel ashamed and remorseful about feeling resentful of their children. For that reason, they don't talk about these emotions. Your parents may hope their silence protects you from the sting of envy and the burden of grief. They may pretend to feel nothing but pure undiluted happiness at your success. As we've seen, however, silence and denial do not eliminate emotions, they amplify them. Grief, resentment, envy, and sorrow will bubble up and trickle out in the form of undercutting comments or half-hearted compliments that leave you feeling betrayed, confused, and unjustifiably attacked at the moments when you hoped to feel most appreciated.

Why Your Parents May Never Thank You

What happens if you express your disappointment and hurt to your parents about their thinly veiled hostility in response to your achievements, if you ask them to thank you for your hard work and sacrifice to fulfill their dreams? Chances are, all hell will break loose. Your parents may accuse you of the very hostility, unfairness, betrayal, and lack of appreciation that you feel *they* are guilty of.

Your parents can't thank you for fulfilling their dreams without acknowledging they had asked you to place their well-being above your own. Not only would most people be ashamed to admit such selfishness, they probably don't believe they acted selfishly in the first place.

Direct Requests

If your parents told you directly what they expected, then they asked you to be *dutiful,* not self-sacrificing, and they view being dutiful as what parents "rightfully" expect of children. Your parents probably think it's immature, unfair, and ungrateful of you to resent your duty. They may never have questioned their own family duties. And they probably don't want to start now. Perhaps they'll ask themselves those questions someday, but they're not likely to do it because you tell them they *ought* to.

Indirect Requests

If your parents communicated indirectly, they probably believe they never asked you to do anything except what you wanted. From their point of view, your adoption of the career of their dreams was entirely your choice. You were *supposed* to be making yourself happy. If you didn't do what they told you to do, how can you blame them? Thanking you for fulfilling their dreams would be equivalent to saying, "I was a bad parent." They probably don't agree, and they certainly won't think it's fair of you to ask them to, especially when they tried so hard not to impose their dreams.

TAKE PRIDE IN YOUR OWN ACHIEVEMENTS

The only surefire way to buffer yourself against your parents' lack of gratitude is to stop asking your parents to thank you, approve of you, or appreciate your struggle. You thereby release yourself from a mighty and fruitless struggle. I'm not suggesting that you won't still want your parents' pride and thanks. Nor that you reject them if they're offered. I am suggesting that you won't get them by fighting for them. And that you're better off learning to appreciate yourself than depending on anyone else's gratitude or approval.

Your best defense against ambivalent praise or devaluing comments in response to your achievements is twofold:

- **First,** make sure your goals are above all meaningful to you, so that your parents' appreciation remains *secondary* to your own pride and pleasure in your success.
- **Second,** realize that your parents' ambivalence reflects grief and disappointment that stem from their pasts. It does not reflect a defect in your ability nor does it detract from your achievement.

What you can and must do for yourself—and what your parents can never do for you—is take pride in your own achievements.

MOVING FROM BLAME TO RESPONSIBILITY

As you understand your parents' influence on your career better, it's natural to wonder "what might have been" if your parents had raised you differently. Whether such questions are fair or realistic isn't the point; you're bound to have them. Thoughts such as these are hazardous only if you allow them to fester into blame:

Why couldn't they have done a better job coping with their own disappointments?

Why couldn't they have stood up to their parents or society?

Why couldn't they have worked harder to be happy so they wouldn't pass burdens on—intentionally or unintentionally—to me?

The Temptation and Limits of Blame

Blame points a finger at and holds a "culprit" in a fixed posture of accountability. For that reason, blame is tempting. Rage finds a clear target. For the same reason, however, blame limits our growth. It shields us from complexity. We can't ask any questions that would muddy the purity of our outrage or bring multiple culprits into view—or worse, leave us with no culprits at all, just a ragtag band of vulnerable and flawed human beings. Letting go of blame means assuming responsibility for your own life.

Letting Go of Blame

Before you can let go, two barriers may stand in the way. You may not feel ready to shift the balance of power with your parents, or you may be reluctant to grieve.

SHIFTING THE BALANCE OF POWER

If you feel that you can't pursue your goals until your parents agree with your plans or apologize for the past, you will feel enraged whenever you think about how they're "stopping" you from doing what you want. Rage at your parents may make you feel powerful, but it doesn't give you power. In fact, it binds you in a childlike dependence on your parents. You've given *them* the power to decide when you can move on. Giving parents this power is dangerous, because as we've seen, they probably don't believe they're stopping you from doing anything or that they have anything to apologize for. And they're likely to believe that forever. Sooner or later, you have to shift this balance of power, declare your freedom, and grow—on your own.

Ironically, waiting for your parents to admit they were wrong keeps you in the role of their protector. Instead of *choosing yourself,* you want to recruit them to your side and bring them along. That way, you won't have to leave them behind, feeling disappointed or frustrated. You must retire from the job of being responsible for your parents' happiness. Not only must you learn independence from your parents, they must learn independence from you, too. It's scary; it's hard; but it's necessary. And it's possible. It's your best and only shot at finding out who you really are. The result makes it worth any amount of effort. Others have done it. So can you.

Finding the Courage to Grieve

In order to grow, you have to shift emotional gears from blame and rage about "what might have been" to sorrow. Grieving clears your emotional closets. If you don't grieve about disappointments now, the emotions won't disappear. You'll simply pass them on to the next generation.

The scary thing about grief is its intensity. If you aren't accustomed to expressing powerful emotions, you may be afraid that you'll get swallowed up by sorrow and won't be able to escape. I have known many people who shared this fear, but I have never known anyone this happened to. To the contrary, the redemptive truth about grief is that it acts very much like a storm front. As long as you allow the rain to pound, the winds to blow, and the thunder to shout, an exhausted but peaceful calm *always* returns.

There will be other storm fronts, followed by other calms—grief is profoundly cyclical. But for that matter, so is life. If you can't run, can't hide (and you can't), you might as well dive into the river of your sorrow. You may be pleasantly surprised at how well you swim, and at the peace that awaits you at the other side.

Part Two

Family Dynamics

✦

4

What Is a Family System?

If you want to understand how the "single thread" of your family's influence on your career connects with the larger pattern of its impact on your life as a whole, this chapter weaves the two together. You will learn what a family system is, how families communicate emotion, and the difference between false and true selves.

A FAMILY SYSTEM IS A WEB OF RELATIONSHIPS

What does it mean to describe a family as a "system"? It means focusing on the web of relationships among its members, who continually interact in verbal and nonverbal ways. From a systems perspective, if you want to understand the behavior of any one family member, you have to understand how it is influenced by—and in turn, influences—the behavior of all others.

Imagine that you want to understand why a child suddenly comes down with a mysterious stomach ailment to stay home from school. Let's say you have ruled out medical causes and negative changes at school as motivations. Viewing the child as part of a *family system,* you ask: *What has happened recently within the family that would make the child want to stay at home?* You then learn that one of the parents is unemployed and depressed. The child's presence at home gives the parent a distraction from worry, companionship, and the chance to exercise a skill—taking care of an ill child.

Symptoms Arise to Solve Family Problems

From a family system perspective, the stomachache isn't just a symptom, it's an *attempt to solve an emotional problem.* Many of our physical and emotional symptoms are just that—attempts to solve emotional problems within our families. Usually, the problems haven't been admitted, talked about, or understood. That's why the symptoms we develop to solve them are so often indirect and clumsy, and may make the problem worse rather than better. Nonetheless, when trouble arises within an individual family member, it ripples throughout the system until other members respond.

THE GUARDIAN AND THE BEAST: A FAMILY SYSTEM ALLEGORY

How do individual family members recognize there is a problem? How do they figure out what to do? The following allegory applies a family system perspective to these questions:

> In an allegory by Plato, the guardian of a big beast observes it carefully. He gradually learns to recognize its desires and irritations, how to approach it, where it should and should not be touched, at which moments it becomes restless or calm, what sounds it makes according to what mood, by which words it is soothed or upset. Consequently, the guardian creates a method out of all these observations: he calls "good" what the beast likes and "bad" what it is disgusted by, and he subordinates his perception of reality to the beast's whims. He then calls his overall outlook "wisdom."
>
> —Piero Ferrucci,
> *What We May Be*

This allegory shows how society teaches us to conform to social norms, and that we forget we were taught to do so. The beast can also be seen as our family—whose care we inherit at birth, whose wounds we attempt to heal, and whose pleasures and pains we sense with uncanny accuracy. Out of these observations, we create a method of behaving that is pleasing to the beast.

We express ideas and feelings the beast likes. We hide those that disgust or upset the beast. We subordinate our inner needs and desires to those of the beast, calling the outcome a self. And in the process, we forget that we were molded. We assume we invented ourselves.

You Are Always Both Guardian and Beast

As an individual member of your family, you are the guardian and everyone else is the beast. But for every other individual in your family, you are part of the beast. To understand your own behavior, ask in what ways you serve as guardian to your family beast. To understand the behavior of every other member of your family, ask in what ways he or she responds as guardian to the beast that includes you and the rest of your family.

Constant interaction—a *feedback loop*—takes place between guardians and beasts. You are always influencing and being influenced by your family system. That larger pattern of influence embraces the thread of your career. When you leave your family and arrive in the work world, don't be surprised when the "beast" appears to have magically transported itself into your workplace—and demands that you serve as guardian. The workplace is a beast, too. When bosses or colleagues resemble your family, you'll feel tempted to play guardian. If, however, you're alert to the presence of the beast, you can recognize when you're being drawn into guardian ways. Awareness breaks the spell.

How You Are Linked to Your Family's Emotions

Your training as guardian began in the fluid emotional environment of your earliest family interactions. In this realm, you are joined with the *emotional system* of your family. You are bathed in a sea of emotions—pleasure, anxiety, fear, approval, attraction, repulsion, joy, or sadness. Waves of feeling circulate among family members. Each person's response stimulates another ripple in the tide, so that a continuous wavelike movement of emotion links the family together.

Emotional Reactivity: You "Conduct" Emotion

You've probably had the experience of walking into a roomful of people and immediately sensing sadness, fear, or anxiety. Almost immediately, you discover similar emotions are triggered in you. This instinctive, automatic detection of and response to emotions is called *reactivity*—the term used by family systems theorist Murray Bowen. Reactivity happens constantly in all relationships, but it's especially intense within families.

Human beings conduct emotions in the same way that metal conducts heat or electricity. Metals don't choose to be conductive;

because of their nature, they are. Similarly, we don't choose to be emotionally reactive; we simply are. We are uncannily sensitive and accurate readers of our families' moods, whether we are aware of their effect on us or not.

Your Compulsory Intuition Registers Truth Deeper Than Words

Not only do we use our five senses, especially sight and sound, to detect emotions, we employ what I call *compulsory intuition* with our families. This instinctive knowledge—or gut sense—registers the truth of what someone is actually feeling beneath his or her words. An anxious tone of voice, a clenched jaw, the barely discernible shift in direction of a pair of eyes conveys a deeper truth about what family members feel or desire from us than what they explicitly say.

What Is a "Family Unconscious"?

Compulsory intuition reflects our linkage with a *family unconscious,* a metaphor developed by psychologist E. Bruce Taub-Bynum. Visualize your mind as a series of concentric spheres radiating outward from the individual. The innermost sphere is your personal unconscious. The intermediate sphere is your family unconscious. The outermost sphere is the collective unconscious.

- Your *personal unconscious* is the territory mapped by Freud, with its id, ego, and superego, a repository for your personal memories and symbols.
- Your *collective unconscious* is the transpersonal realm explored by Carl Jung, connecting each individual with the vast expanse of human history in the form of shared archetypes and symbols, revealed through dreams, imagination, myth, art, and religion.
- Your *family unconscious* connects these two realms of the mind. It includes your family's memories, dreams, hopes, losses, and achievements. It connects you with your ancestors as well as current generations of your family.

Your Family's Psychic Field Works like a Magnet

How are you linked to your family's unconscious mind? After all, it's invisible, without physical substance. Taub-Bynum suggests the link is created through a field that works like gravity or electromagnetism. These forces do not concretely exist. They reveal their presence by the impact they have on objects affected by the field. You can't see a magnetic field. But you infer its presence when metal shavings are moved close enough to a magnet to be drawn toward it.

Think of your ancestors' lives generating a psychic or emotional field of family patterns that connects you to the past and is transmitted to each new generation by the preceding one. Each generation, in turn, contributes new memories and knowledge to the field. When you think of your family's emotional system as a field, influencing you before you were born, it's easy to understand why family patterns and expectations are so persistent and powerful. You are tuned in not only to your parents' and grandparents' lives, but to a vast web of earlier family relationships and memories.

For help exploring your family's history, see **Exercise 15-1.**

Why We Feel Pressure to "Soothe" the Beast

Pressure to soothe the "family beast" affects everyone. It is especially strong for children, who can neither run nor hide, and have no defense against it. But why is soothing so compelling? Why can't you just let the beast howl?

There are two reasons why the pressure to soothe your family is so strong.

- **First,** you are physically and mentally hard-wired to be emotionally reactive to your family. It's hard work to shut down these "circuits."
- **Second,** family members instinctively try to maintain stability within the system. This homeostatic tendency regulates the emotional temperature of your family in the way a thermostat regulates the temperature of a house. When stress and anxiety—perhaps the most contagious of emotions—disturb family members, others automatically try to calm them and restore the status quo.

WHAT ARE FALSE AND TRUE SELVES?

Whenever you soothe your family by speaking or acting in ways that deny or distort your authentic beliefs or desires, you act as a false self. You cover up your true self. The danger of pretending to be a false self is that you may act your role so well, you begin to fool yourself—you forget that you are acting. Playing a role may be easier and cause less trouble than expressing the real you. Like an actor leaping off a stage in mid-dialogue, you'll fear the consequences of abandoning your role, especially if your family's been giving you rave reviews.

Your true self may linger silently inside for years. You can refuse to explore it or express it. You can hide, neglect, and defy it. What you can't do, however, is obliterate it. Over time, it will tug, nag, shout, or scream for your attention. Not because it wants to make trouble. But because it's who you really are. At that point, you will have to decide whether to continue acting a part, or to live your life as yourself.

DEFINING YOUR TRUE SELF

How do you define your true self? How do you distinguish who you are from who your family needed you to be? The longer you've been fused with your family beast—trapped in "emotional stuck togetherness," to use Dr. Bowen's apt phrase—the more confused you're likely to be about where your own and others' feelings begin and end. You don't have a buffer to separate you from family members' anxiety, anger, sadness, or depression. You'll feel pressured to meet their needs, since you feel them almost as urgently as if they were your own.

Self-Reflection Reduces Emotional Pressure

Fortunately, your true self isn't completely defenseless against the pressure to soothe the family beast. You may be wired to react instinctively to the moods of the beast, but you're also wired for self-reflection. You can become conscious of your emotions, and make thoughtful choices instead of reacting instinctively. Such awareness counterbalances emotional pressures. It can prevent you from drowning in your family's sea of emotion.

Slow Down Reactivity and Differentiate Feelings from Thoughts

The more you practice slowing down your emotional reactions, the better you will become at objectively observing and learning from your own and others' feelings. Instead of emotions controlling your behavior, you decide how to cope with and express them. The thoughtful pause between emotion and reaction—between lifting a fist and slamming it on a table, between feeling afraid and running away—enables you to differentiate what you are *feeling* from what you *think* about it.

In that pause, you create true freedom: the freedom to decide what you will say or do. Taking time to make deliberate, reflective choices enables you to differentiate your true self from false selves constructed under emotional pressure. After all, you can't decide if actions reflect your true self until you've taken the time to go inward to ask.

GETTING UNSTUCK FROM FAMILY CONSTRAINTS

Differentiating thoughts and emotions does not mean you get rid of feelings. On the contrary, it enables you to tolerate intense emotions without being taken over or bossed around by them. You can respond to others' feelings while remembering that they aren't your own—that you're a separate person. The capacity to step back, observe, and learn from your own and others' emotions gives you the psychic solvent to get "unstuck" from family constraints. With this freedom, you can make choices and take stands that reflect your authentic values and goals.

The Worst and Best News About Defining Your True Self

Defining your true self requires enormous emotional courage. You have to stop asking yourself what others expect or approve, and instead ask, "Is this right for me?" or "Is this what my true self is calling me to do?" It requires hard work, the willingness to take risks, and the resilience, strength, and stamina to constantly grow and change. You have to stand up for yourself even when you must do it alone. You have to discover your unique interests, dreams, and talents, even if they've been covered up for a long time. Worse yet, not only do you have to define who you are, you have to speak and act upon this knowledge. You have to align your everyday life with your true self.

The worst news about defining a self, however, is the same as the best news. Ultimately, *you don't have a choice.* This difficult, relentless search for self-knowledge is the only path to maturity, emotional health, and wisdom. The path may be steep and littered with barriers, but if you want these rewards—and it's next to impossible to live happily without them—you must keep climbing until you get there. When you arrive, you'll know who you are. There is no greater reward.

5

Redefining Family Love and Loyalty: Breaking the Cycle

As you define your true self and break the cycle of hand-me-down dreams, you disrupt family patterns. In response, you need to prepare for predictable emotional hazards. Your family may welcome and support changes you initiate. If so, they're probably accustomed to your independence, and are confident in their own. If they aren't sure they can get along without you, however, they may fear your growing independence. But they probably won't say they're afraid. Instead, they'll accuse you of these misdeeds:

- You are being unloving and selfish.
- You are dishonoring your parents and abandoning your duty.
- You are disloyal to the family; therefore, the family is justified in punishing you in whatever way it takes—from refusing to talk to you to cutting you out of a will—to force you to "come to your senses."

LETTING GO OF FEAR, GUILT, AND ANXIETY

You're likely to react to such emotional heavy artillery with fear, guilt, and anxiety, and perhaps with second thoughts about disrupting the status quo. Nonetheless, once you've discovered you have a true self—even if you aren't sure of the details—it's impossible to pretend false selves are anything else. You can't go backward, even if that's what your family asks. You have to let go of fear, guilt, and anxiety, and defend yourself instead.

Your Best Defense Is to Listen Carefully

You may be tempted to refuse to listen to dramatic accusations of unethical, callous behavior on your part. The best defense against them, however, is not to cut off or rebel against your family, but to listen carefully to them and consider the fears and assumptions their judgments are based on. Then decide whether you agree with the accusations. If you don't, define the ethics of your behavior in your own terms. Even if no one else in your family agrees with you, clarity about your principles will increase your strength and confidence.

For more on the consequences of cutting off or rebelling against your family, see **chapter 6.**

OVERTURNING MISGUIDED ASSUMPTIONS ABOUT FAMILY LOVE AND LOYALTY

The accusations at the beginning of this chapter follow from three widespread but misguided assumptions about family love and loyalty, which also determine and justify the "rules" for loving and loyal behavior. If you overturn the assumptions, you can change the rules without feeling guilty. The three misguided assumptions are:

1. Children belong to their parents.
2. Love equals sacrifice.
3. Loyalty means protecting your family from change.

1. Children Belong to Their Parents

What do parents have the right to expect from their children? Society views children as "belonging" to their parents until they reach an age determined by law. At that point, they belong to themselves. In effect, parents own their children. They are empowered by law to determine where, with whom, and how their children live. These laws shield children from responsibilities they aren't prepared to exercise, but they also give parents control over every aspect of their children's lives. It's not surprising that some parents view their children not just as their physical and legal property but emotional and psychic property as well.

Children Are like Wax—They're Supposed to Fit the Mold

Some parents define their job as molding children to fit their standards and expectations. They assume that children are like wax; as they grow, they should naturally fit the mold parents outline for them. If they don't, children are rebelling against their duty to grow as they "ought to." Parents then feel cheated, betrayed, and outraged by their offspring's refusal to comply with the unwritten contract that binds children to do what their parents demand.

If a child grows up deficient in the parents' desired degree of attractiveness, intelligence, charm, or success, parents blame the child. The child they have has deprived them of the child they "deserved" to have. Parents view their children's individuality as defiance. They feel denied the reward they're entitled to in exchange for raising children: seeing them turn out as expected. Disappointment—in the child and in the experience of being a parent—cuts deep in the heart of parent and child.

INDIVIDUALITY IS NOT DEFIANCE

Individuality isn't defiance, of course. It's essential, universal, inevitable. You can't help being unique. As your life unfolds, you discover what your interests and talents are; you don't decide what you want them to be. You can't force-fit yourself into someone else's mold. If you try, it will only be an act. You cannot belong to anyone else, even as a child. Children have limited legal rights, but their identities belong to themselves from birth. It seems like an obvious truth. Why is it sometimes hard for parents to see it?

I DID WHAT MY PARENTS WANTED; NOW IT'S YOUR TURN

When you can't see something obvious, emotions block the way. You must need not to see it so much that it disappears from view. A generational chain reaction kicks unfulfilled dreams down the family tree in both direct and indirect forms. To the extent that your parents force-fit themselves to meet their parents' needs, the unexplored and unfulfilled parts of themselves will seek expression through you.

Your parents will feel entitled to your behaving dutifully toward them as they did toward the preceding generation. This expectation will be inextricably linked in their minds with the values of showing respect for elders, honoring parents, and showing gratitude for the gift of life.

Do Parents Seek Payback? Or Ask for Healing?

Your parents' expectation that you can and should become the person they want you to be stems from two powerful hopes:

- **First,** that you will validate their behavior. You will confirm the wisdom and righteousness of each generation fulfilling the dreams of previous ones rather than "selfishly" pursuing their own.
- **Second,** that their dreams will finally come true through you. However unrealistic this hope may be, it is blindingly powerful.

Do these hopes suggest that your parents seek compensation—payback—from you for what they gave to your grandparents? Or that they seek healing for lost dreams? Ironically, parents often demand the former as a cover for the latter.

Equating Honor with Obedience Creates Conflict and Confusion

Parents' request for healing usually isn't deliberate or direct. Their hurts and hopes telegraph throughout the family's emotional system seeking children who hear, care, and respond. Describing parents as seeking healing from their children, however, runs counter to most people's beliefs about what is supposed to happen in families.

Parents are supposed to nurture and heal their young, not the other way around. The idea that parents seek nurture and healing from children is so shameful to most people, they deny it. An effective way to deny something is to call it by a different name: in this case, parents don't seek healing, they claim entitlement to respect, honor, gratitude—which children fulfill when they do what their parents ask. Honor, respect, and gratitude—undeniably positive values in all human relationships—are equated with obedience, thereby providing parents with a rationale for blaming children if they refuse to fit the mold.

Obedience is not the same as honor, respect, or gratitude. Equating these values simply covers up parents' underlying request for healing. It also sows seeds of conflict and confusion. Your parents feel insulted and betrayed when you turn out differently from what they asked for. Their vision is clouded by emotional needs. They can't see that you're simply living your life according to what *you* think is right. You, in turn, feel hurt when your parents are disappointed in you, and you are astonished and dismayed that they can simultaneously accuse you of being unloving while they say and do cruel things that show how conditional their love really is!

You Belong to Yourself

If your family accuses you of unloving treason when you strike out on your own, you may find strength in the following antidotes to this accusation:

- **You don't belong to your parents.** You never have, don't now, never will. They are not entitled to ask you to alter your identity to meet their needs.
- **Your parents' judgments are distorted by their emotions.** You can't judge your behavior based on their anger and disappointment.
- **Love is not obedience, neither is respect.** You are not being unloving or disrespectful when you do what you think is right.
- **Your family's accusations don't necessarily mean they don't love you.** They do mean that they confuse love with being entitled to control your life. They therefore see no contradiction between loving you and behaving in unloving ways. You can distinguish love from control, and acknowledge the presence of both in your family's behavior. Losing illusions about family love is painful in the short run, but in the long run yields clarity and freedom.

2. Love Equals Sacrifice

When you were growing up, did your parents admonish you to behave with reminders of the following?

- The privileges they've given you that they never had.
- The relative ease of your life compared to the hardships of theirs.
- The sacrifices of time, energy, and money they've made to raise you.
- The extent of their love and devotion as parents—which their sacrifices prove beyond a doubt.

These comments reinforce a common but dangerous equation between love and sacrifice. Love is measured by the sacrifices parents make for their children—of personal happiness, financial resources, time, and hard work. Parents sacrifice themselves to provide their offspring with privileges and opportunities they never had. In return, they expect children to demonstrate their love by expressing gratitude for these sacrifices and by taking full advantage of the privileges and opportunities they've been given.

If Love Equals Sacrifice, Can Sacrifice Stand In for Love?

Each generation should prepare the next generation to attain a higher standard of living.

Many people believe that working toward the financial betterment of the next generation is the most important duty of a parent. Although it skews the goal of raising children in a material direction, this definition provides a practical, clear-cut job description for many parents. It not only equates love and sacrifice, it suggests that the most important sacrifices—signs of love—parents make involve money.

The danger of equating love with sacrifice—especially monetary sacrifice—is that it becomes a stand-in for love. Parents can use their sacrifices as bargaining chips to coerce children into gratitude, compliance, and good behavior. Children, in turn, can turn their parents' ammunition against them. By comparing their family's standard of living unfavorably with those of others, they can manipulate parents into guilt, shame, or perhaps prod them into more and greater sacrifices on their behalf. Where does it end? What happens to love?

When Love Equals Sacrifice, It Becomes Tangled with Resentment and Rage

Parents who have sacrificed their lives for their children feel they have bought the right to their children's compliance, gratitude, and love. They feel resentful and enraged if their children "cheat" them by failing to keep their end of the bargain. Children have two choices. They can break the deal, receive their parents' righteous wrath, and risk losing their love. Or they can buy their parents' love with compliance—and, in turn, look for compensation for their sacrifices from the next generation. Equating love with sacrifice keeps the generations knit together in an endless loop of mutual obligation. What it doesn't do, tragically, is enable anyone in the family to feel loved.

How Sacrificing Differs from Giving

Sacrifice and giving differ both in their motivations and in their emotional impact. Sacrificing isn't the same as responsible nurturing and protection of children. Nor is it the same as voluntarily giving to those you love. Instead, it is the chronic and persistent habit of making others' needs more important than your own because you'd feel guilty and ashamed to do otherwise.

Sacrifice differs from giving in these ways:

- It doesn't feel like a choice but a burden.
- It doesn't spring from generosity but from moral duty.
- It doesn't create pleasure or fullness but depletes you.

By contrast, choosing to act responsibly enhances self-esteem, self-respect, and pride. Choosing to give returns pleasure and feelings of connection with others. In both cases, you end up with more than you started with, even though you've given something away.

How Sacrifice Creates an Altruistic Paradox

Those who sacrifice don't feel the satisfaction of giving freely to others. Those who are "sacrificed for" don't feel they've received a gift. Instead, they have incurred a debt—one they didn't choose and must repay on someone else's terms. Psychiatrist Richard Allen describes these results as an "altruistic paradox." At both ends, sacrifice leaves resentment—not love, generosity, or kindness—in its wake. It's a moralistic, martyred, meager substitute for love, too contaminated with craving for recognition and compensation to fool anyone into believing it's really love.

Love Does Not Equal Sacrifice

You may not be fooled by sacrifice masquerading as love. But if your parents accuse you of "unloving," "selfish," or "ungrateful" behavior when you defy their wishes, you may nonetheless be tempted to comply with their demands. If you've grown up equating love with moral duty, you'll have a hard time letting family members view your behavior as self-seeking treachery. Bear in mind, however, that your own sacrifices are just as much substitutes for love as your parents' were. Love does not equal sacrifice. Sacrifice corrodes love. You will end up resenting anyone who demands that you demonstrate love by giving away control over your life.

Genuine Love Demands More and Returns More Than Sacrifice

Genuinely loving your parents demands more of you than sacrifice. It requires that you struggle to know yourself, that you bring your life into alignment with that knowledge, and that you not allow your family's accusations of "unloving behavior" to lure you into betraying yourself. Resist capitulating to emotional blackmail. Your parents' sacrifices can't be paid back, not by you or anyone else—they can only be mourned. And they, not you, must do the mourning.

You don't have to either agree with or fight back against your family's accusations. If you can remain true to yourself without running away or caving in, *that* is truly loving your family. They may never recognize or thank you for it, but you will know the truth. This kind of tenacious, sturdy, demanding love strengthens you, makes you more independent, and enables you to develop maturity and courage. In the long run, it does not leave rage or resentment in its wake but compassion and wisdom, which you gain through learning how to give it. You will always gain more, never less, from giving genuine love. Love has *nothing* in common with sacrifice.

3. Loyalty Means Protecting Your Family from Change

Has your family ever used threats to persuade you to back off from plans of action or to coerce you into silence? Did they . . .

- Cut you off from financial or other forms of family assistance?
- Threaten never to speak to you or include you in family gatherings?
- Spread rumors about your motivations to extended family members or friends so they, too, would cut you off?
- Promise to hold you accountable if certain family members "have a heart attack and die" because of your behavior?

Threats like these spell out the stakes if you continue with your plans. They also clarify that the price of disloyalty to the family will be the end of family loyalty toward you.

What's wrong with this picture? Can family members possibly hope that threatening you will increase your motivation to please them? Isn't demonstrating the flimsiness of their loyalty to you an ineffective strategy for commanding greater loyalty from you? What can they be thinking?

BUYING PROTECTION—FAMILY STYLE

In movies about the mob, buying protection means making payments in order to guarantee your safety to the very people who are threatening you with violence in the first place. In families, the motivation for buying protection is emotional, not monetary. But efforts to intimidate family members into backing off from changes that disturb the status quo share this ironic twist with the mob kind: the payoff your compliance buys is the continuing goodwill of the family members who are threatening to make you suffer in the first place.

They feel justified in threatening you because you have exposed the family to dangerous change. You've broken the code of family loyalty. If you're allowed to "get away with it," others might try. The family might change so drastically, it would never be the same. They are protecting a "way of life."

FEAR OF CHANGE SPURS ATTACKS ON LOYALTY

Fear of change spurs the attacks on your loyalty. Underneath this fear is often genuine concern that long-hidden family problems may be exposed to the light of day, and that some members may not be ready or able to cope with disappointment, depression, isolation, or other kinds of emotional fallout triggered by the changes you want to make.

Trying to stop change by hurling fire and brimstone at anyone who tries to nudge the boulder of family "loyalty" may not be a constructive, realistic, or effective strategy for coping with change, but it is common. At one time or another, we've all tried this strategy for one compelling reason. Anything else—talking about the fear, assessing the pros and cons of change, figuring out what to do next, all of these constructive, realistic responses have a huge downside: they themselves not only begin but advance the dreaded change!

ANYTHING THAT DOESN'T STOP YOU MAKES EVERYONE STRONGER

To sustain your strength and confidence in the midst of attacks on your loyalty, prepare yourself for blaming responses from family members who view your behavior as dangerous. Remember that the basis of their hostility is fear, and that the strategy of hurling fire and brimstone is instinctive. It indicates the depth of their fear. Even family members who should know better, who understand that hiding from change never works, may elect to circle the wagons anyway, because fear of change is more powerful than common sense.

Like the proverbial killing of the messenger, when you are perceived as the bearer of bad news, family members will . . .

- Try to silence you. If silencing you doesn't work . . .
- They will slander you. If slander doesn't work . . .
- They will punish you. If punishment doesn't stop you from changing, eventually . . .
- The family will have to change, too.

Take Heart in Knowing You're on the Right Track

In the meantime, keep in mind what family therapist Murray Bowen said of the slander family members hurl when individuals define true selves: If you aren't hearing accusations of unloving, selfish, ungrateful behavior, you have probably been sidetracked, and you're not taking a stand that will help yourself or your family learn to live more independently. If you *are* hearing them, take heart in knowing that the work of defining your individuality, messy and painful though it can be, is indeed getting done. It will benefit you and, in the long run, everyone in your family.

TO LOVE AND BE LOVED AS YOUR TRUE SELF

The greatest benefit of overturning these misguided assumptions about love and loyalty is that you thereby rebuild the meaning and purpose of love within your family. Not a love based on fear, mutual indebtedness, guilt, and sacrifice, but on fairness, honesty, and acceptance of one another as you truly are—not as others need you to appear to be. Holding out for this kind of love requires steadiness of purpose on your part. It means not accepting *as love* love from your family that requires you to pretend to be someone else.

Acceptance Must Work Both Ways

Acceptance works both ways: not only must you insist upon being known and accepted as you are, you must also know and accept your parents and other family members as they are. This doesn't mean that you have to accept disrespectful or hurtful behaviors from family members. You have the right and the responsibility to limit such behavior. But you do have to stop wanting or waiting for your parents to change their behavior to make it easier for you to do what you want, say what you think, be who you are.

Acceptance of each family member as an individual—warts and wonders all—transforms love within your family by distinguishing it from threats, fear of punishment, manipulative guilt, and control. When you remove these distortions, you can see your family members as people with whom you can choose what you say, do, confide—or not—just as you do in other voluntary relationships. You can exchange real gifts. You can love and be loved as your true self. That is the ultimate goal of breaking the cycle of hand-me-down dreams, and the reward that makes it worth your time and effort.

6

When You Rebel Against or Cut Off Your Parents

Sometimes our parents' most significant influence stems not from efforts to fulfill their dreams, but from trying to cut them off or rebelling against them. It's tempting to believe we can find the freedom to be ourselves by becoming detached from our families. Often we justify these strategies with such wishful thoughts as: "If I rarely see my parents, I'll stop feeling hurt and angry." "If they don't know what I'm doing, they won't have the chance to criticize me." "I will never be anything like my parents because I'm doing the opposite of what they did." "My parents don't have any influence on my career because I never talk to them."

These are wishful thoughts because these strategies don't work. Rebellion always derives its shape from the family being rebelled against. Rather than giving us independence, rebellion ties us to our families as closely as yin to yang. It doesn't diminish our parents' influence, it intensifies it. And cutting off our parents simply transfers the problems we have with them to other relationships—especially to the next generation.

WHY REBELLING DOESN'T WORK

Rebellion is triggered by feelings of constriction. It's like being zipped into a suit of clothes that is too tight; instinctively, you want to bust loose. Once you do, you'll remember how cramped you felt, and you'll be wary of letting anyone zip you into anything similar ever again. Although many people equate busting loose with freedom, they aren't the same. Busting loose is only a precursor to freedom. True freedom means finding a suit of clothes that you decide fits, not seeking the opposite of the constricting one you hated. Ironically, the opposite keeps you bound to the suit that bedeviled you in the first place.

That bondage is a clue to the underlying purpose of rebellion. Like a shadow cast on a wall, your rebellion takes the shape of the underside of your parents' dreams—dreams they disapproved of or disowned. And your parents will probably disapprove just as hard when you bring these embarrassing or shameful dreams to light. After all, if they thought these were safe, ethical, or noble dreams, they would not have disowned them in the first place.

Nonetheless, your parents will find relief and release in your rebellion. They'd be reluctant, however, to admit such guilty pleasure. You, too, may be reluctant to admit that your rebellion is tied to your parents' needs, because you've probably felt the brunt of their disapproval most of your life. Such reluctance does not prove detachment—to the contrary, it suggests the intimacy of the tie.

It Takes a Martyr to Raise a Rebel

This alliance between rebellion and parents' cast-off dreams sounds tricky, and in some ways it is. But in other ways it couldn't be simpler. For example, we've all seen parents who bawl out their children for disruptive or defiant behavior while simultaneously reinforcing it. Imagine a mother driving a car who orders a child in the backseat to stop eating a bag of candy. The girl ignores the commands, and tells her mother to "shut up." The mother angrily threatens to stop the car and discipline the child, but doesn't. At the end of the drive, the child skips from the car and the mother cleans up the candy wrappers, complaining bitterly about how selfish and rude her child is. What has the child learned?

It's obvious to any outside witness that the child has learned she can get away with disrespectful and defiant behavior. Allowing a child to get away with such behavior is tantamount to encouraging it. The little girl knows that she can safely tune out her mother's verbal criticism. She isn't really supposed to change her rebellious behavior, just to feel guilty about it—although she probably won't. Because, you see, although neither of them could put it into words, their behavior reveals that the girl and her mother agree perfectly on one thing: the daughter's task is to get exactly what she wants in life, and her mother's mission is to help her get it.

Why would a parent encourage selfish, defiant behavior? Chances are that in the daughter's selfish behavior lurks the hidden demon of her mother's long-suppressed defiance. This mother has probably been forcing herself all her life to be polite, responsible, dutiful, and reliable—not because she wanted to be, but because she felt she had to be. She has, in short, never busted loose. Nor has she ever grown past busting loose to consciously choosing exactly how polite, dutiful, and reliable it is healthy and wise to be.

The child's rebellion is to disobey; the mother's is to encourage her daughter to do so. Neither recognizes the choreography that links their behavior. The mother will criticize her daughter for disrespectful, disobedient behavior. And in response the daughter is likely to become more boldly defiant, especially during adolescence.

The mother will feel unappreciated. The daughter will feel harassed. Eventually, the daughter will flee to find freedom from her mother's criticism. Later, in her career, she'll be determined not to become "trapped," "tied down," or a "martyr" like her mother. She'll seek a level of freedom, self-expression, and autonomy that her mother would never dream of—because it's so "irresponsible" and so "selfish"—except, of course, that her mother did dream. The daughter's rebellion makes her more like her mother than her mother ever allowed herself to be. Over time, however, she'll have to make sure that her efforts to be unlike her mother don't prevent her from discovering who she herself really is.

What Criticism Really Tells Children

When parents stridently criticize their children, it's equivalent to saying, "Here, I'll give you something you'll have to flee." Such parents are feeling pinched by lives that constrict them. Feeling pinched and not knowing how to bust loose turns people into dissatisfied human beings and critical parents. Indirectly, they bust loose by encouraging their children to break the rules. But they can't admit to doing so without breaking the rules themselves.

If your parents were chronically or harshly critical of you—or if their discipline was erratic—they probably secretly resented the standards and rules they insisted you should follow. If they'd felt confident and happy with rules they had chosen, they wouldn't have criticized or threatened you, they'd simply have enforced fair and consistent standards, which would have ensured your compliance. It would also have encouraged you to seriously consider adopting your parents' standards as your own later on.

Children aren't stupid. If your parents were angry, bitter, or vindictive, they were hardly an advertisement for the benefits of following their example. Your parents can insist they were only trying to help you to benefit from rules and standards that served them well. But you are not going to believe them. Instead, you're likely to want to get away and stay away. The irony is that your parents probably wish they could, too.

Don't Settle for Busting Loose

You can rebel against your parents at any age—whenever you break rules you inherited rather than chose. But remember, it's just a first step. Don't settle for busting loose or for being anyone's opposite. Go on to create your own rules. If you do, you won't get stuck in the anger and contempt for your parents that launch most rebellions—and keep people stuck in them. As long as you're rebelling against your parents, you haven't explored new territory, just the forbidden fruits of your parents' banished dreams. Remember, if your parents had known how to find freedom and happiness, they would have. Use their example to find your own freedom. And then, just maybe, your parents will learn from yours.

When Hand-Me-Down Dreams Become Nightmares

Hand-me-down dreams can sometimes play out like nightmares. If your parents were pinched hard by life, they may have been left with the urge to pinch back. If they haven't found constructive outlets for these impulses, they may pinch back through you. When parents seek revenge or vindication through their children, the interactions between them are similar to those described above, but the stakes are higher. In such cases, rebellious behavior can lead not just to criticism and conflict, but to patterns of self-defeating, self-destructive, or dangerous behavior, as demonstrated in these two brief examples.

> At hockey practice, a father whose son has been disciplined by the coach for losing his temper and hitting a teammate on the head with his stick advises the boy, "Charley, take it easy. These other kids are too delicate to take a licking. And the coach is so fussy he'll toss you from the game. Cool it a little."

What does Charley learn? He *doesn't* learn to resolve disputes peacefully, or to respect his teammates and his coach. He *does* learn that his father equates aggression with strength, and feels contempt for both the rules of fair play and those who enforce them. To earn his father's respect and to avoid the dreaded adjectives "delicate" and "fussy," Charley will have to demonstrate contempt for the rules and for authority, and to act aggressively, without regard for the feelings or safety of others.

Later in life, Charley may act aggressively not only on the playing field, but with his teammates and bosses in the workplace. And when he's "tossed from the game" at work for hostile behavior, Charley will probably blame the exaggerated sensitivities of "wimps" and "wusses" for his problems in playing fair. Unless he changes his own attitudes and behavior, Charley will pass on hostility, contempt for weakness, and desire for revenge to the next generation.

> A girl brings home a math test with a D and a note from her teacher requesting that her parents call to set up a conference. To reassure Marlene, her mother tells her only nerdy girls do well in math, and that pretty girls don't need "book smarts." Her father tells her the teacher is a moron, and he'll indeed call her up, but not to confer, to "give her a piece of his mind."

What does Marlene learn? She *doesn't* learn to value her intelligence or her education, to try hard, or to view teachers as sources of knowledge and help. From her mother, she *does* learn to doubt her intelligence and to value looks as her most important asset. She learns from her father to view authorities with fear and suspicion, and when problems arise, to seek protection rather than solutions.

Later in life, Marlene may find it hard to feel smart or act smart in the workplace—and she'll feel competitive with and critical of women who do. She'll rely on her appearance, not her competence, to create positive impressions. And instead of seeking mentors who can teach her how to set goals, work independently, and challenge herself intellectually, she'll seek women who can soothe her feelings and men who will "fight" her battles. Like Charley, unless Marlene changes these attitudes and behaviors, she'll pass on to the next generation her self-doubt, her distrust of authority, and her dependence on others to solve her problems.

If your parents "pinched back" at other people through you, they probably treated you like Marlene's and Charley's parents did—in ways that undermined your self-esteem, derailed your social skills, or rewarded you for self-defeating or aggressive behavior. Nonetheless, your parents would probably deny that they set out to harm you. If your parents were "pinched hard" by their own parents, all they knew was pinching back. In their own minds, they weren't being mean-spirited or teaching you maladaptive coping skills, they were teaching you about life. The world they grew up in, in short, is the only world they knew. It isn't so much that your parents didn't know better, but that they didn't know anything different.

You Can Begin New Patterns for Future Generations

But you do know differently. As with hand-me-down dreams, you can shake off hand-me-down nightmares as well. Being pinched and pinching back is a chain reaction that links generations within a family, and keeps them trapped. Like a chain, no matter how strong it looks, the power of these self-defeating patterns can be destroyed by removing a single link. Every time you recognize and rectify a distortion in the way you cope with aggression, authority, or the rules of fair play, you not only break the chain, you begin a new pattern for future generations to build upon. These new patterns will dramatically improve your chances for finding fulfillment in work and harmony in your relationships with others.

WHY CUTTING OFF DOESN'T WORK

Perhaps you never see your parents, don't ask them for anything, don't talk to them, and never call or write. Doesn't such lack of contact evolve into independence over time? If you've spent years without knowing anything about your parents, and they know nothing of your life—or at least nothing important—aren't the tethers of family influence finally broken?

The logical answer might appear to be yes. But the truthful answer is no. Our emotional entanglements with our family members follow a logic that is derived not from our outward verbal or physical contact with them, but from the implicit, inward impression they made upon our minds. Two rivers, for example, may pour their waters into different seas separated by vast geographical spaces, but their tributaries forever link them to a common source.

Cutoffs are an extreme form of rebellion. Like rebellions, they can sometimes be useful as a springboard to independence and freedom, but they should not be mistaken for the ultimate goal. Rebellion produces a mirror image of your family—a way of life your parents desired but didn't approve of. Cutoffs, by contrast, produce not a mirror image of your parents, but a frozen slice. The shape that's been "iced" reflects not a cast-off dream, but one too painful to bear, so that it's shrouded in numbness—and mistaken for dead.

Just Because a Dream Is Frozen Doesn't Mean It's Dead

Cutoffs are fueled by hurt and rage—two emotions as difficult to untangle as blue from the sky. Ironically, the purpose of cutting off is to adopt a stance of calm and cool toward your family. If you're cut off from your parents, you may disclaim their power to make you feel anything, much less such powerful and vulnerable emotions as hurt and rage.

Your disclaimer may echo those your parents have made to you about family members they have "lost touch with," or "don't know anything or care anything about." Cutoffs, like rebellions, are passed on from one generation to another. In the emotional logic of families, however, the extent of hurt and rage floating around the family tree can be calculated by the amount and duration of distance required to sustain the "chill."

The dreams, hopes, and hurts your parents put on ice are revealed by the age at which you had to run, where you ran to, and what you ran away to do. Usually, the timing and purpose of your flight echo dramas begun but not resolved by earlier generations of your family.

For example, in his late teens Alex stormed from his father's house, shouting, "I'll never be back. And I'll never be a boring old fart like you." He joined the merchant marine and sailed around the world for a decade. When Alex was in high school, his father always spoke contemptuously of his son's love of adventure novels and of his dreams of travel to exotic places. He advised Alex to study accounting and prepare himself to "get a real job."

Alex left home at the age his father had been when he decided to major in accounting—at his own father's urging. The only lingering clues to his father's youthful dreams were his outbursts at moments of frustration while Alex was growing up. "Someday," he would mutter bitterly, "I'll take off to where none of you will ever find me . . . to Timbuktu, or the shores of Labrador."

Without being aware of it, Alex's father as much as painted an exit sign for his son. Alex witnessed his father's dissatisfaction with his own choices. "Getting a real job" didn't lead to inner peace. He also heard his father's fantasized solution: to flee so far away that family could neither find nor follow him. The fantasy of escape shared by father and son suggests another shared belief—that the gravity of family expectations is so strong the only way to be yourself is to physically relocate to a safe distance. If your family can't see you and you can't see them, perhaps the gravity will diminish. Alex's father was never brave or reckless enough to flee. But he fears that his son will be. And the fear itself becomes Alex's prod to leave.

When Alex's father sees him reading adventure and travel books, it triggers his contempt. Contempt is a cover for fear. Whatever endeavors our families have taught us are beneath us, are unworthy of a member of our gender, our family name, or our heritage are precisely the ones they're secretly afraid will tempt us away from the serious-worthy-respectable-appropriate occupations that family duty and continuity require. Our parents understand the temptation, because they have felt it themselves, and have buried it deep inside. The greater the temptation, the more intense and vocal will be the contempt.

The greatest danger Alex's father confronts isn't his son's quest for adventure. It's the danger that his own frozen desires will thaw and twitch to life, bringing with them conflict, disappointment, and pain. Criticizing and pushing Alex away keeps his own desires frozen and helps him to regulate his pain. Alex, in turn, is hurt and enraged by his father's contempt and distance. He, in turn, holds his pain at bay by distancing himself from his father.

Distance Does Not Mean You're Indifferent

If, like Alex, you are cut off from one or both parents, you may find safety in the coolness of distance. Detachment protects your parents from reminders of their own cutoff desires. And it protects you from the coldness of your parents' criticism. Ironically, you may all claim the purpose of distance is not to protect you from pain but simply the result of indifference. "What do I care what *he* or *she* is up to? After all, *he* or *she* doesn't give a damn about me!"

This claim will keep you calm and help you feel justified in maintaining your distance. Indeed, there are periods in life when we all need some distance from our families. But at some point, if you want to know yourself completely, you'll have to thaw out your emotions about your parents. At that point, it will be important to recognize that, as useful as this claim of indifference has been in the past, it is also a far-fetched lie that has never fooled anyone but you.

Like Flies in Amber: How Cutoffs Freeze Relationships

Obviously, far from dying, frozen dreams acquire a prolonged shelf life. If you cut off your family because you have goals, relationships, or values that your parents refuse to acknowledge or actively criticize, then you've probably also tried to freeze the hurt and rage you feel in response. You probably think that your parents don't know the real you. And you're right. But what you may not realize is that you don't know them either—at least not fully. When people freeze up around one another, rigidity is all they see. The result is that everyone misses out. You won't be able to express your own vitality and richness to your parents, nor will theirs be available to you.

No matter how contemptuous or oblivious your parents may seem in your presence, the truth is that something about you scares them. Your personality, values, or ambitions remind your parents of parts of themselves that are deeply frozen. As we've seen with Alex and his father, when your parents' frozen dreams confront the warmth of your potential, the danger of emotional meltdown will preoccupy and distract them from seeing you clearly. They can't afford to divert their attention from controlling and reversing the thawing process. So, like Alex's father, they'll behave in critical or dismissive ways that prompt you to exit, vowing never to return.

If you don't return, you'll never see your parents change. Like flies in amber, they will remain frozen in time as the people they were at the age you withdrew—as you will to them. Forever critical, forever a threat. Should you meet them later in life, you may be surprised at how they've changed, yet amazingly, they treat you as though you haven't. And they'll feel the same way about you.

Thaw Yourself Out First

The only way to overcome the great divide is to thaw yourself out first. Cutoffs provide an artificial immunity to being hurt by your parents. Distance can't heal hurt and rage; it only diverts your attention and temporarily numbs you. Genuine immunity comes first from admitting to yourself how much your parents' criticism or detachment really has hurt you over the years. Second, it comes from cultivating the courage and strength to be yourself even if it scares your parents and turns them into bullies. Understanding that you *scare* your parents may not stop them from trying to hurt you, nor will it always stop you from feeling hurt, but it does steal the moral high ground away from them, and with it much of their power.

WHY BOTHER TO MEND CUTOFF RELATIONSHIPS?

If you remain cut off from your parents, you freeze not only your relationship with them but your own emotional development. We grow and change through our connections with other people. If you never see or talk to your parents, you'll never struggle through the conflict, hurt, forgiveness, understanding, insult, injury, outrage, and compassion that would enable you to stop being their children and become their peers. Nor will they be forced to see you as an independent adult rather than a child whom they must guide and rule.

Not only do cutoffs give your parents prolonged power over you, but by freezing your emotions you will repeat their pattern in your own life. Sadly, you will need to protect yourself from the warmth and vitality of your own children, just as your parents did with you. Your children will aim for the frozen turf inside you like guided missiles. They'll want *all* of you, just as you wanted all of your own parents. And they'll instinctively try to open up whatever is shut down. They will force you to pay attention by resurrecting those closed-off places in their own lives. They will understand better than you how badly you need the meltdown. And if you can't find a way to accept what they have resurrected, then they may pull back from you. Not because they want to, but because it hurts too much to bump up against *your* rejection.

There Are No Shortcuts to Self-Discovery

As liberating as it might initially feel to aim at being unlike your parents, at some point you have to discover who you truly are on your own. You have to open up the vast middle road between polar opposites and explore your own values, dreams, desires, and goals. If you don't, you're likely to feel trapped and frustrated, out of touch with what authentically excites you. And if *you* don't determine what excites you, your children *will,* and will demonstrate it for you, just as Alex did for his father. Children will perform this service even if it is dangerous, even if you disapprove.

On the other hand, if you cut off your family, imagining you are thereby pursuing an independent, completely self-determined life, a part of you will remain frozen in time at the age you were when you cut off. The emotions that you shut down will remain frozen until the next generation melts them down and pours them out.

Rebellion and cutoffs, in brief, do not provide shortcuts to self-discovery. They simply divert it to the next generation. If we want to find out who we are as individuals rather than as reflections of past generations, we have to admit that our families have influenced us. We have to sort out what fits and what doesn't, and toss away whatever constricts us. We have to figure out what we want to do, and commit ourselves to doing it. Finally, we have to tell family members what we're doing, and then hold fast to our goals even in the face of criticism or doubt—our own or theirs. Each of these steps is difficult and sometimes harrowing. But each is also possible. And each is worth the effort, because we become our true selves by trying.

7

The Influence of Sibling Order and Gender

If you've ever constructed a family tree—or a genogram—you've seen how family relationships diagram across space and time. These diagrams record the dates of births, deaths, marriages and remarriages, and geographical origins for your ancestors. The earliest ancestors appear at the top of the page like an upside-down bulb, planted in the past, from which subsequent generations radiate downward like the branches of a tree.

You can visualize in a family tree the web of marriages, divorces, births, and adoptions that connects you to previous generations. These are the facts of your family's history. But to visualize your emotional connection with your ancestors, you need to add another dimension: *purpose.* How has each generation of siblings added to the strivings of earlier generations? What were they trying to achieve? And how has your work been influenced by everyone else's?

To visualize this dimension, imagine a vast chandelier, with a lightbulb radiating white light in the center. The lighted bulb is surrounded by spherical rows of *unlighted* bulbs of every imaginable color. The white light in the original bulb contains all the wavelengths of the color spectrum, but in potential form. The chandelier isn't whole until all the colors are lit. The middle bulb's job is to radiate light onto as many unlighted bulbs as it can, and to stimulate those bulbs to radiate as many different wavelengths of light as possible.

Those bulbs, in turn, shine their light on the next row of bulbs, and so forth, until a vast rainbow of purer and purer beams of light radiates outward. If you chart the relationships among the bulbs physically, it looks like a family tree. But if you look not at the separate bulbs, but at the light itself, it's one huge, holographic rainbow. This is the living pulse of family history. And each family's purpose is to build the brightest, most colorful rainbow they can.

Parents act like the middle bulb of the holographic chandelier. They strive for wholeness. To begin with, parents choose each other for this reason. Romantic love is driven by the hope that someone else can fill, complete, or heal us. Of course, this rarely happens. Even when it does, it may not last. And there are almost always empty places left over. These untapped potentials, unfulfilled dreams, and unfinished conflicts press for expression through the next generation.

Depending upon the available workforce of siblings of various ages and genders, parents will assign children various tasks (or "wavelengths") until as many needs as possible have been met. These assignments are not formal, explicit, or even necessarily verbal. But they are nonetheless clear. Parents assign jobs through the selective attention, approval, or relief they telegraph emotionally in response to their children's behavior.

Two parents may feel different degrees of satisfaction with themselves, their lives in general, and their relationship with each other. Usually, the parent who feels least satisfied—and most urgently in need of help—will determine the first child's "assignment." Sometimes the next child's, too. Sometimes parents take turns. (If they can't take turns, the resulting conflicts breed triangles, which are discussed in **chapter 8.**) As each child is born, she or he inherits the next unfilled task.

BIRTH ORDER AND SPECIALIZED JOB ASSIGNMENTS

The "color of light" parents nurture in the first child expresses their most compelling need or hope. This may be to fill in gaps in their own lives, such as lack of education or financial success. It may be to develop practical or emotional caretaking skills the family needs to remain stable and solvent. Or it may be to vicariously fulfill long-deferred dreams of professional or creative achievements.

If the first child rises to the task, the parents are relieved of pressure, and can nurture the next most pressing "wavelength" in the next child, and so forth. As with any labor force, children specialize. As each sibling's "job" is clearly established, no other children perform the same task. Older children absorb the most immediate tasks. Younger children absorb those that remain. And only children must scramble to fill them all.

From Oldest to Youngest: How Responsibilities Evolve

Parents with numerous children construct broad rainbows of light through their children. Stereotypically, the older children are viewed as most responsible and the youngest as least responsible. Younger siblings don't necessarily have less responsibility, however; they simply have less urgent or less specific tasks. If older siblings have already earned the law degree that eluded a father or achieved the journalism career that a mother began but never finished, younger siblings can pursue lower priority but still important tasks—tints and hues that fill in the undeveloped colors of the family's holographic rainbow.

Parents also change as they mature, in midlife and later years. As they become more secure—professionally and personally—these changes alter their expectations of younger children. They may discover opportunities to express their own potential, to achieve deferred dreams, or to accept themselves as they are. Parents who never had much money or freedom in their youth may find themselves encouraging younger children to spend and explore. An older sibling who was encouraged to save and achieve may look upon these "indulgences" with envy and resentment, even though these seemingly easier tasks are still part of the family's larger quest for completion.

Younger siblings in turn often envy older siblings their greater authority and responsibility within the family. They may also envy older siblings' independence from aging parents, whose fear of being left without children to care for—or alone with each other—usually lands most powerfully on the youngest child.

For the most part, older, middle, and younger siblings all assume the other's job within the family was more rewarding. Each sees in the other's "hues"—ranging from achievement to delinquency, responsibility to self-indulgence—the unfulfilled potential that their own family "job" restricted them from expressing. And, of course, it is precisely the unfulfilled potentials, regretted most passionately, that will become their most urgent dreams passed on to children of their own.

Why Can't My Parents See **All** *of Me?*

As each child is born or adopted into the family, some of his or her potential talents and personality traits will be highly relevant to the parents' needs. Some will not. The constellation of skills and traits anticipated from each child will vary depending upon the family's current economic and psychological condition, as well as the talent already available to the family team. For that reason, parents often fail to see the wholeness each child embodies.

Caleb was the second son in a family of three siblings. His older brother, Ivan, was always touted as "the brain" in the family: "He's going to be a Civil War historian like Shelby Foote." Caleb was "the athlete": "He's going to be the next Roger Maris." His younger sister, Katy, was known simply as "our sweet little girl." Caleb excelled at sports, but he also got good grades. Sometimes his report cards were better than Ivan's. Katy brought home the best report cards of all. But the only "brains" that seemed to matter to their parents were Ivan's—his were the only report cards posted on the refrigerator, the only ones bragged about to family friends.

Caleb felt furious at his parents for not recognizing his academic achievements. For a while in high school, he deliberately brought home bad grades. But all his parents said was, "Well, son, it's a good thing you've got a strong right arm." Eventually, Caleb went on to earn a Ph.D. in chemistry. But his parents still introduced him as "the son who could have been a professional athlete," while they referred to Ivan, who dropped out of a graduate program in American history, as "our son who nearly finished a Ph.D." Katy graduated from college summa cum laude, but her parents introduced her as "our little girl who is going to give us beautiful grandchildren someday."

How can parents be so blind? Are they deliberately trying to hurt, humiliate, or insult their children? How could they not understand that an athletic child also has a brain, that a child with a brain might not want a Ph.D., and that any child has more purpose in life than to produce grandchildren for her parents? Although it hurts children enormously when parents don't see all of them, this narrow vision usually results from the parents' own frustrations, not conscious malice.

The Light of Your Parents' Imagination Forms a Halo Around You

Caleb's father, for example, had grown up as one of eight children, and started working in an automotive factory when he was sixteen. He read constantly, but never graduated from high school. He lived in the same town all his life. He never traveled. Never got a college degree. He was a blue-collar worker with white-collar aspirations. He admired Shelby Foote more than anyone. And after him, Roger Maris. But he admired Shelby Foote *more.* His most urgent need was a son with a "brain" who could study history. His next priority was a son who could hit home runs.

Caleb's mother, by contrast, had been satisfied with her roles as wife and mother. All she ever wanted from her children was grandchildren. These desires focused on Katy, not "the boys," whose futures "belonged" to their father. From their parents' perspective, it would be a duplication of precious and limited family talent to have two or three brains in the family, when they needed one Shelby Foote, one Roger Maris, and one mother of grandchildren.

Caleb's father had been dutiful and hardworking all his life. His blindness to his children's wholeness duplicated his own parents' narrow vision of his possibilities, which he in turn cast upon his own life. He never imagined himself going to college, writing books, or playing sports. It was only after he had his own children that his imagination opened up—and with it, compelling dreams for his children's futures that obscured his vision of the actual children standing in front of him.

If your parents' "job assignment" for you highlighted only one of your abilities, then indeed they didn't see all of you. Like Caleb's father, the light of their imagination blinded them. That single quality shone like a halo around you—it filled in the talents or achievements your parents needed to feel complete. To them, it's your most outstanding feature. They won't view it as your "job assignment," however, but as the natural dispersal of family gifts that they have simply observed in you and your siblings from birth. It will seem obvious to them that you are naturally "the smart one," "the kind one," "the troublemaker," or "the most mature." And they'll probably assume it's obvious to everyone else, including you.

Breaking the Mold

The sibling "duty roster" aims at psychological economy by parceling out specialized jobs among siblings. But it suffers from built-in inefficiency. Since jobs are assigned according to which sibling shows up (i.e., is born) in time for the vacancy, rather than according to ability or interest, mismatches will frequently occur. These may be mismatches between the child's aptitudes and the job requirements, or the child's personality traits and those required to succeed in a particular endeavor. For example, Ivan loved history as much as his father did. He was smart enough to earn a Ph.D., but he hated structure and deadlines. Much to his father's chagrin, he left graduate school to work as a house painter and read history in his free time.

There's another inevitable problem in the sibling duty roster. Parents who strive for completion through their children will discover at some point that their children seek completion for themselves. We may be one among a row of unlighted bulbs to our parents, but we're all "middle bulbs" to ourselves. We contain the white light of many wavelengths of talents and desires. Over the course of our lives, we'll strive to develop not just the one quality that completes our family's rainbow, but as many tints and hues of our own as we can.

If you try to break the mold of your parents' expectations forcibly—as Caleb did when he deliberately brought home bad grades—you may hit a wall instead. Rather than forcing his parents to recognize both his intelligence and his athletic abilities, Caleb discovered that his parents pushed back against his expansion, like a constricting mold.

If you've bumped up against the invisible shield of your parents' narrow expectations, you've no doubt felt frustrated, alienated, and angry. And most difficult of all, like a person walking down a hall shouting while no one seems to hear, you may have doubted yourself. Do you really have a voice? Were your parents right? Are you perhaps not as smart as you hoped?

Such frustrations contribute to long-lasting hurt and distance between parents and children. Often they prompt the cutoffs and rebellions described in **chapter 6.** They also contribute to anger and resentment among siblings. The child whose report cards go unnoticed will resent the child whose report card *is* fussed over. The child whose stories are not read aloud will resent the child whose stories are. The child who has remained a dependent adult companion to aging parents will resent the child who has achieved professional and financial success outside the family. These resentments can run deep and fester over time.

Create Your Own Job Description

The only way to break the mold of constricting family job assignments is to quit working for the family firm and become self-employed. You can't wait for your parents to notice you have a brain or a degree or a Pulitzer Prize. You can't wait for a sibling to resign so there's an opening for the job you always craved. You can't stretch your old job description. You have to start from scratch and create your own. Make sure it's flexible. Make sure it's open-ended. Make sure you report to yourself. Because when you're walking down that hall shouting, it's *yourself* that you must hear. *You* decide what's real.

The benefits of writing your own job description are multiple. First of all, over time, your parents and siblings may learn to see not only you more clearly but one another as well. If so, everyone's job may allow for greater flexibility. Next, you'll become your own rainbow. You will grow by unleashing as many desires and talents as you can. And finally, the more you explore your individuality, the more likely you are to know your children's. You won't be blinded by the light of your imagination; you'll see your children as the intricate, intriguing and unpredictable beings they truly are: just as you were when you were a child, even if no one ever said so; just as you are now, even if you're just finding out.

GENDER AND JOB QUALIFICATIONS

Gender serves as an occupational qualifier or disqualifier for family job assignments. In Caleb's family, being male served as a *qualifying* gender for the priority role of "brain" given to the firstborn, just as Caleb's and Katy's gender qualified them, respectively, for the job of athlete and nurturer.

If Katy had been born first, however, her gender would have disqualified her from the job of "brain" as long as sons were anticipated. If no sons arrived, her parents would have to decide whether or not gender would continue to serve as a qualifier. The strategies parents use to negotiate a mismatch between a family's "duty roster" and the genders of available children vary according to how rigid the parents' own gender roles have been.

Looking Outside the Family

If your parents believed in strict rules defining appropriate "masculine" and "feminine" behaviors and personality traits, they won't encourage you to defy those norms. Not only would they find such cross-gender behavior morally suspect, they might also feel angry and resentful at watching you "break rules" that they themselves diligently followed. Ironically, the more sternly they admonish you to "be a strong boy" or "be a good girl" the more they reveal two things—their anxiety about gender roles and how much work they require to maintain.

If no girls or boys are available for the needed job, parents will often look outside the family for a child of the appropriate gender to mentor. A father may disappear with the Boy Scouts every weekend, or a mother may "borrow" a niece. Sometimes, parents will seek a child of the desired gender to adopt. Sometimes, parents will postpone filling the job until the spouse of a grown child becomes available. In such cases, men usually provide business, professional, or financial skills. Women provide nurturing and communication skills. Sometimes, a parent may feel such urgency to have a child of a particular gender that he or she divorces and remarries in an attempt to reproduce the right gender.

Such substitutions create complicated rivalries and deeply hurt feelings among siblings. They underscore for the "disqualified" children that their gender renders them insignificant, irrelevant, or incomplete in certain ways in their parents' eyes. If your parents disqualified you for certain family jobs because of your gender, you may harbor lingering resentment of the restrictions your gender placed upon you, lingering fear of behaving in ways your parents would call "unmanly" or "unwomanly," and lingering doubt about your ability to perform skills ascribed to the other gender.

To heal such painful legacies, remember that your parents' view of gender reflects no real limitation of yours; it reflects their own divided minds, their own painful legacy of rules and restrictions. You don't have to be bound by these. You can't afford to get stuck trying to fulfill anybody else's vision of what a man or woman should be. The range of what men and women have in common is vaster than our differences. What matters is what we choose to do with our talents and goals—not how many people of the same gender share them.

Daughters as Sons; Sons as Daughters

In some families, a mismatch between job openings and gender may lead parents to bend the rules for one or more children. A daughter may be given privileges usually reserved for sons, or vice versa. Given current sexist attitudes, however, while parents might describe a girl as acting like a son, they would rarely describe a boy as acting like a daughter—unless it were a deliberate insult. They're more likely to describe the boy as ambiguously "special," or simply not comment on the arrangement. After all, to call a girl a tomboy implies grudging respect, but to call a boy a sissy is demeaning. For the boy or girl encouraged to cross the gender barrier, this freedom is a mixed blessing. The rules haven't been tossed out, only bent.

Marta was the middle daughter of three born about eighteen months apart. She became her "father's only son" when he realized her mother wasn't going to have any more children. A contractor, her father took her to construction sites and taught her building trades. Marta enjoyed being allowed freedoms her sisters didn't have, such as wearing pants and sneakers, using tools, and visiting the lumberyard. However, she didn't enjoy hearing her skills commended as "good as a boy's." Nor did she enjoy being admonished not to "cry like a girl." Nor did she enjoy incurring envy and hostility from her sisters and her mother at having been singled out for special rules and respect.

Being a "good son," even if you're a girl, in other words, can be as restricting as it is for a boy. Marta, like others in this dilemma, is caught in a no-win situation. To accept praise for being "as good as a boy" means accepting that being a girl is inferior. Does Marta act like a boy in order to win her father's praise? Or does she act like a girl in order to be true to her own gender? And when, pray tell, does she get to act like herself?

Claim the Freedom to "Act Like"—And Be—Yourself

Therein lies the problem with using gender as a qualifier: even when the rules are bent they still apply. Stereotypes about masculine and feminine behavior lead parents to measure children against external standards. Children are seen as fitting or not fitting norms, even when girls are measured as sons or boys are measured by "feminine" standards. Children will grow up trying to "act like a man" or "act like a woman" rather than trying to "act like" either themselves or whole human beings. It's only when you claim the freedom to do this latter, however, that you can discover what it means not to "act like," but to *be* a man or a woman—on the inside, where it counts.

HOW CHILDREN SABOTAGE GENDER ROLES

No one grows up unaffected by gender roles. The first question anyone asks a parent about a newborn is, "Boy or girl?" Families have always been responsible for enforcing compliance with gender roles. For this same reason families also inevitably foster sabotage. Earlier chapters in this book describe how children scan their parents' lives for imbalances, missing pieces, and suppressed desires and will try to compensate for these imbalances in their own lives, often without the foggiest notion why.

The more polarized parents' gender roles are, the more they are likely to demonstrate such imbalances. Men with a strong need to appear masculine are usually attracted to women with a strong need to appear feminine, and vice versa. The contrast between the partners shores up their gender roles rather like a neutral mat around a brightly colored painting. However, the shoring up also limits each person. Stereotypically, the male role stifles emotional expression and intimacy, and the female role stifles assertiveness and autonomy. Children who witness such imbalances will strive to rectify the balance.

Timothy's Story

Timothy is the twenty-year-old son of a wealthy corporate lawyer. His mother is a full-time homemaker. As a junior in college, Timothy became too restless to concentrate and flunked out, ruining his chance of being accepted into law school. He was tested for learning disabilities or other physical contributors to his restlessness, but all were ruled out.

Tim's father is driven and ambitious, stressed to the point of a vulnerable heart. He had been absent during most of the important events of his children's lives. Nurturing was left to Tim's mother. Although Tim's father was affectionate with his daughters, he finds it impossible to hug Tim. His own father had been rigid and demanding with him, and he reassures himself that fathers should not be too soft with their sons or they will be ill prepared for the harsh competitiveness of a "man's world" in later life.

Timothy, by contrast, is spontaneous with his emotions. He openly offers and asks for affection. He works as a peer counselor at a counseling center and does volunteer work tutoring elementary school kids. He says he wanted to become a lawyer just like his father until his mysterious "restlessness" disrupted this plan. When his father warns him about the dangers of "idleness" and "drifting," Tim agrees. He feels bad about disappointing his father, but says he "just can't seem to find the motivation" to plan a career. He feels stuck and confused. And his father feels frustrated and worried. Both are puzzled over how different they are from each other.

It isn't puzzling at all when you view Tim's behavior as a commentary upon his father's life. Tim's *behavior*—not his words—holds a contrasting mirror up to his father, with the masculine polarities reversed to highlight what his father would describe as feminine values and traits. It's as if Tim were saying, "Here, Dad, is what is missing in your own life. Get a clue."

Melinda's Story

Melinda is a thirty-year-old investment banker, the oldest of two daughters born to a father who was a military officer and a mother who had worked at a bank before she married. After Melinda and her sister began grade school, their mother wanted to return to work part-time, but her husband forbade it. He announced that the roof over their heads and the clothes on their backs belonged to him, because he paid for them. And therefore, his wife and children would have to obey him, or else. Melinda's mother complied and stayed at home.

When Melinda was growing up, her mother would tell her funny stories about customers at the bank, about the broken-down old Buick she used to drive to work, and about gossipy coffee breaks with the "punch card girls." Although her mother insisted she was happy with her life as a mother and homemaker, the animation and wistfulness in her voice when she spoke of her life as a young, independent "career girl" belied her claim.

Melinda grew up determined she would never allow any man to control her life. She graduated at the top of her college class, earned an MBA, and went to work on Wall Street, where she has thrived. Her career has been all-consuming, however, and she rarely has time for friends, much less romance.

Moreover, Melinda doesn't like investment banking. She does like the money it brings her, however, and she cannot imagine earning less. As Timothy did for his father, Melinda mirrors her mother's imbalances, with the feminine polarities reversed to highlight what her mother would describe as masculine attributes.

FREEDOM FROM STEREOTYPES: FINDING MIDDLE GROUND

If you witnessed ways in which your parents' rigid gender roles constricted their freedom and happiness, then you may also have set out to sabotage the rules—either deliberately, like Melinda, or without fully understanding your rebellion, like Timothy. Simply reversing your parents' gender roles can constrict you as much as your parents' roles did. Eventually, you have to risk something more daring—releasing gender roles altogether.

Timothy and Melinda need to find the middle ground between polarized definitions of masculine and feminine. Tim needs to invent something that eluded his father, a balance of family, friendships, and work he cares about. Melinda needs to create the same balance, although she begins her journey toward middle ground from the opposite end. To invent that balance, they have to start not from gender but from scratch—the unsifted richness of their own "ungendered" inner potentials.

The Greatest Mischief of Gender Roles

Perhaps the greatest mischief caused by rigid gender roles is the way they teach us to undervalue and overvalue different aspects of ourselves. Typically, girls learn to undervalue boldness, self-assertion, and independence, and to overvalue nurturing, compromise, and caretaking. The problem is that *all* these traits in balance are essential to a complete and healthy individual. Typically, boys are taught to undervalue empathy, emotional expressiveness, and interdependence, and to overvalue competitiveness, power, and aggression. The problem is that *all* these traits in balance are essential to a complete and healthy individual. Gender roles, however, force us to choose.

Refuse Forced Choices and Create Your Own Middle Ground

When your career path echoes these "forced choices" between masculine or feminine goals and behaviors, then going to work every day becomes an exercise in self-oppression. Choosing a job because it fits your own or your parents' image of what male or female work should be can keep you busy, may even lead to profit and success, but it cannot make you happy unless it also fits with *who you really are*—which is always quite different and much more complex, creative, and interesting than any gender stereotype. The only possible choice is, therefore: *Refuse to choose.* Instead, insist upon creating your own middle ground.

8

Triangles: When Parents Choose "Special" Children

Parents don't always agree on the goals they ask their children to achieve. If yours didn't, you had to choose between them. Alternatively, one of your parents may have paid lots of attention to your academic performance and your career plans, while the other parent either seemed indifferent or paid more attention to your siblings. Both situations involved you in *triangles.*

TRIANGLES: SHIFTING ALLIANCES AMONG FAMILY MEMBERS

A triangle is a relationship among three people, two of whom are allied as insiders, and the third distanced as an outsider. Sometimes, the third "leg" of a triangle isn't even a person, but an activity a person is so absorbed in that it effectively shuts out his or her partner and their children—this can range from work or sports to television, surfing the Net, or drugs.

Triangles involve not just parents, but all family members. If, for example, you are especially close to your mother, then your father and siblings are outsiders to you two insiders. But if another sibling is especially close to your father, then your mother and the rest of you are outsiders to this alliance. All of you are involved in a series of interlocking triangles.

Members of each triangle are sensitive to the movements of all others. If, for example, your "outsider" father sought you out for special attention, this shift would ripple throughout the interlocking system. Everyone accustomed to being insiders with you and your father would suddenly feel like outsiders, and would seek each other out for new "inside" relationships. Triangles, like waves in the ocean, are always there, but always changing shape.

Unresolved Conflicts Lead to Triangles

Families often view triangles not as choices but as predestined bonds. They may describe particular children as born to be special to one parent because they are "so much alike," or because their birth order or gender "causes" the deeper connection. (See **chapter 7** for more on birth order and gender.) Children may well be born into triangles, but they are never the initiator of a triangle.

Parents entangle children in triangles because these triangles help parents to resolve conflicts. Parents who struggle for power in their relationship may covertly seek the upper hand by asking a child to become an ally. Or, a parent who feels deprived of affection and warmth may seek intimacy with a child. To retaliate, the other parent may bond closely with another child. These alliances grow stronger with time, because they temporarily relieve the initial conflict.

Unresolved conflicts are ubiquitous in families, and therefore so are triangles. They stabilize relationships that, like a two-legged stool, could not stand without a third leg. Triangles are tempting because they maintain stability, and because they are accomplished quickly—without the need for forethought or difficult conversations. We're all so familiar with the strategy that when conflict arises with one family member, we automatically seek out another to confide in and "take our side." However, triangles only siphon off tension. Shifting alliances between insiders and outsiders shuttle tension around the family, but they do nothing to resolve the root conflict between two parents, and harm the children caught within them.

WHEN CHILDREN ARE FORCED TO CHOOSE

An only child, children of parents in conflict, and children of divorced families often find themselves forced to choose between their parents. This is agonizing for a child for obvious reasons and for some less obvious ones. The most obvious hardships are distance from the parent you didn't choose; feeling responsible for pushing the parent away; and feeling guilty for making the parent feel that you love him or her less—although that is almost never true.

Alfred's father pressured him to do well in science and math so Alred could become an engineer, as he had done. Alfred's mother encouraged him to read poetry and history. His father thought liberal arts were "squishy" and "feminine." His mother thought engineering was for "hacks." Each parent interpreted their son's pursuits in the other's domain as a personal affront. Alfred didn't want to choose sides, but he didn't know how *not* to. Ultimately, he chose engineering, not because he loved it, but because his father's scorn for the "effeminate" humanities was harsher and harder to bear than his mother's distaste for the "vulgarities" of technical education.

Alfred knew his mother assumed he had chosen his father over her because he loved him better. She also assumed that Alfred shared his father's contempt for her greatest passions. Alfred felt guilty, but he was also frustrated by her assumptions. They weren't true. He had "chosen" his father not because he loved him more than he loved his mother, but because his father's punishment was worse. Alfred knew that his father would withdraw from him completely if he chose his mother, whereas his mother might feel hurt, but she would never cut him off.

This is perhaps the least obvious but most painful dilemma encountered by children forced to choose. They know their parents view the choice as one of love and loyalty, but from their perspective, these are not the criteria. Children are financially and emotionally dependent. They have to pick the parent whose absence would hurt the most, or who they know will make their lives most miserable if they *don't* get "chosen."

Alfred's father was pleased and proud that his son chose to follow in his footsteps, but Alfred never felt warmed by this pride, never felt confident of his father's love and esteem. He knew it was brittle. His father never asked him once throughout his life if he was happy as an engineer. And Alfred knew that if he left engineering to do something else, his father would never forgive him.

Forced Choices Aren't Choices at All

If you were forced to choose between your parents, then chances are you were left with one parent who distanced you, assuming you loved him or her less, and another parent who assumed you loved him or her more—and who confused your fear of losing him or her with your having chosen that parent over his or her partner.

Ultimately, the most devastating harm done by being forced to "choose" between parents is that you wind up isolated, not able to trust either parent to know and love you as yourself.

Both of your parents were so blinded by their power struggles with each other (whether they were married or divorced) that they failed to see the unfairness and harm of your position. As painful as it is to recognize how self-absorbed your parents were in forcing you to choose, it's liberating to understand that you never were choosing. *Choices* are made freely, and you were not free.

You were simply doing your best to survive. You can, therefore, throw out any lingering guilt, as well as any responsibility for taking sides in unfinished battles between your parents. Your greatest responsibility now is what it should have been when you were growing up—to follow your curiosity where it leads you, and then to authentically choose for yourself what you want to do.

BEING SPECIAL TO MOM OR DAD

In many families, children have "special" bonds with one parent but not the other. The special child receives more time, attention, approval, or affection. Sometimes higher achievements and greater discipline are required of a special child. Sometimes standards are lower, and rule breaking is indulged. These variables reflect the specific hand-me-down dream the child has been chosen to fulfill. Sometimes a parent "takes" a special child, focusing attention on the child from an early age. Sometimes a parent "gives" a child to his or her partner, encouraging an alliance that wouldn't otherwise cement itself.

"Special" Bonds Are Neither Natural nor Inevitable

Whether "giver" or "taker," parents tend to describe these affinities as the natural result of biological or psychological imperatives. "Of course girls are closer to their mothers and sons to their fathers." Without pausing to blink, the same family member may later claim, of another relationship, "Of course there's a special bond between girls and their fathers and boys and their mothers."

Alternatively, family members will describe special bonds as the result of shared genetic traits, greater need on the child's part ("He's such a sensitive child, he needed the extra attention . . ."), or a deep but inexplicable rapport between the two. All of these explanations make the imbalance in the parents' affection and energy appear to be either the child's fault or the result of circumstances beyond a parent's control.

They are neither. Special closeness with some children—and distance and neglect for others—are neither natural nor inevitable. What's truly inevitable are triangles. Adults include children in triangles in order to gain control, boost self-esteem, or gain affection, among other reasons. Justifications of special bonds as natural gloss over the adult's responsibility for forging triangular alliances with children. They distract attention from two distinct problems: First, they block parents from seeing that they are using their children to take care of their own emotional problems. Second, they distract parents from attacking their problems directly—in ways that might actually solve them.

The Price of Being Favored

Being a parent's favored child might appear to be an enviable position. It's not. Cheryl, for example, was doted on from birth by her mother. A floral designer before she married, her mother had given up work when she married a banker. When Cheryl was born, her mother finally had someone with whom she could share her delight in the arts, and her criticism of her husband's "Philistine" tastes. Cheryl's father withdrew from both his wife and daughter, spent more time at work, and seemed actively jealous of his own daughter.

Fearing she had pushed her husband so far away he would either divorce her or have an affair, Cheryl's mother "gave" him their next daughter, Peri, encouraging her husband to tutor her, describing her as having a "banker's eye for details," and suggesting that Peri would follow in her father's footsteps. It worked. Cheryl later became an interior designer, while Peri became an investment advisor. Their parents managed to remain married, but both had their closest relationships not with each other, but with their daughters.

Both daughters, however, paid the stiff price of losing a parent—who not only withdrew from them but resented the closeness they had with the partner. The adults acted as though it were the child's presence, not their own communication problems, that caused them to be distant from the partner. "Special" children thus bear the brunt of being scapegoated by their own parents.

Being special is burdensome in another important way. If you're valued by your parent not for who you are but for how you make him or her feel, then you're likely to remain special only as long as you agree to keep doing the things that make your parent feel that way. It's a constraining job, with rigid expectations. Cheryl, for example, discovered that every time she tried to approach her father for advice about money or careers, her mother would become irritable and withdrawn. She never felt free to explore her relationship with her father, or any interests that smacked of "Philistine practicality," lest she lose her special status with her mother.

Becoming "Special" to Yourself

Of course, that's exactly the risk "special" children have to take if they want to claim their adult lives. Far from preserving what is truly special and unique about you, getting trapped in "special" bonds with a parent makes your uniqueness harder to find. You have to retreat to ordinary closeness—which includes struggle and misunderstanding and connection with both your parents—before you'll have the emotional freedom to find not what makes you special to your parent, but what makes you special to yourself.

HELL HATH NO FURY LIKE A SIBLING SCORNED

Triangles create devastating mischief for siblings. Brothers and sisters blame each other for the distance they experience from the parent who withdrew from them. Children understand only that a sibling is receiving affection, time, or approval from a parent and that they are not. Even if the attention is negative—such as verbal or physical discipline—children instinctively understand that their sibling has been invested with emotional importance that they don't have. They don't know what triangles are. All they feel is the loss of a parent's attention, and they respond with envy and hostility toward the sibling who has what they're missing.

Frequently, parents try to quell sibling rivalry by insisting that they treat their children exactly the same. Often, this reassurance only inflames children's jealousies. Children are always more influenced by their parents' behavior than their words. Realistically, parents can't help treating children differently a great deal of the time, given children's different ages and personalities. If children perceive differential treatment but are told it doesn't exist—or by implication, that *they* are wrong, ungrateful, or selfish to mind—not only will they resent the criticism, they'll hold their siblings accountable for yet one more insult to their pride and self-esteem.

Why Sibling Rivalry Is So Durable

Envy and hostility among siblings in response to unequal distribution of parental love in childhood can last a lifetime. Even after adult siblings mature enough to understand intellectually that their parents—not their siblings—were responsible for instigating and sustaining triangular alliances, the emotional scars from years of feeling bitter, betrayed, and deprived can prove difficult to heal. In addition, if you always felt rejected by one of your parents, you may prefer the pain of bickering with siblings to confronting the deeper loss of a parent who withdrew from you.

Ultimately, it's worth the effort to trace sibling rivalry back to the early triangles that drew us into insider or outsider status with our parents and made enemies of our brothers and sisters. Alliances and enmities are dangerously limiting. To find out who we really are, we have to freely explore how we're different from our allies, and what we may have in common with our enemies. Claiming this freedom is the first step in dissolving the triangles that ensnare you.

DISSOLVING TRIANGLES

It's easy to summarize how to dissolve triangles: develop a one-on-one relationship with each and every member of your family, regardless of your past history of slights, awkwardness, rivalry, or outsider status. It takes a lot of guts and tenacity to follow through. But it's possible. And the rewards are tremendous.

You may have to give up being special to one parent, but you'll be free at last to find greater closeness with the other. Being honest about who you really are with each of your parents—indeed, with everyone in your family—takes courage and effort. But it will also deepen your emotional maturity and make you strong and independent. It's only when you feel strong and independent that you can experience authentic closeness with family members. Otherwise, they don't know who you really are. They know only the person you pretend to be because you're afraid to lose them or make them angry.

Developing new interests and goals naturally fosters the process of dissolving triangles, because when you change, everyone close to you has to change, too. Anything restrictive in the relationships will be stretched and will have to become more elastic, or snap. As you change, you may be astonished to discover what you have in common with family members you'd assumed were your opposites, and how different you are from family members with whom everyone always assumed you were "so alike."

For every family member who may be frightened or disapproving of your changes, there are likely to be others who will be inspired by your example to stretch, grow, and claim their own individuality as well. In this way, your efforts to change have the potential over time to liberate everyone in your extended family from the constricting alliances and enmities caused by triangles.

9

Fitting In: How Class, Race, or Feeling Different Influence Career Dreams

What does it mean to be mainstream, average, or normal in a multicultural world? Although a global economy has made these words harder to define, the image of *normal* and *mainstream* most of us grew up with was white, middle-class, college-educated, English-speaking, and white-collar. To diverge from these categories meant you were "different," and being different meant you didn't fit in.

THE IMPACT OF DISCRIMINATION

Not fitting in meant that employers, educators, and co-workers may have discriminated against your family, sometimes in deliberate and systematic ways, but more often through informal means. People in positions of power and privilege advance the careers of those around whom they feel "comfortable"—usually those from similar backgrounds—and exclude those around whom they feel uncomfortable. Such choices are so common, so casual, so routine, they're rarely called discrimination. In fact, groups that have been discriminated against, once they acquire power and privilege, often close ranks and develop their own networks to help advance the careers of people like themselves.

There may be many ways in which your family didn't fit in. Although the social norm of a nuclear family with two heterosexual, married, white, able-bodied, college-educated, middle-class parents has been outdated for a long time, it still holds sway in the popular media as representing average or middle America. It is, therefore, easy to feel different. All you need are family members who are adopted, disabled, gay or lesbian, single parents, poor, who hold orthodox or radical religious or political beliefs, have recently immigrated, or are not native speakers of English.

If you grew up in a family whose class, race, or other type of difference meant that your parents and grandparents were discriminated against, its history obviously affected the educational and occupational choices available to you. This chapter can't do justice to the economic and social consequences of discrimination, but it will explore how your career may have been influenced by your family's *feelings* about being different, specifically whether they view barriers to success as permanent or as temporary—until *you* break them.

WHEN BARRIERS TO SUCCESS SEEM PERMANENT

Some families have been so deeply wounded by discrimination that the barriers to educational and professional advancement seem permanent. If your relatives witnessed generation after generation receiving unfair treatment and getting stuck at the bottom of the economic ladder, they may have concluded there was no hope. "They"—the powers that be—will never let you get ahead.

Resignation and Exhaustion

The consequence of viewing economic barriers as permanent is resignation. If no family member has succeeded in breaking through economic and educational barriers, it will seem foolish and naive to think you can. Even if you make it a little bit further than past generations, you will never receive a completely fair and equal chance.

Don't Try, You'll Only Get Hurt

If your family views encouraging you to work toward educational and economic advancement as setting you up to get hurt, they'll discourage your ambition. Your efforts will only remind them of their own past disappointments. They may believe the wisest course is to diminish your expectations, and to find what solace you can in family and friendships or other areas of life where discrimination is less likely to affect you.

You—Not Your Family—Must Decide What's Worth Trying

If your family has been drained by years of an uphill struggle against discrimination, their resignation and exhaustion are warranted by their experience. All of us may reach points in life when the better part of valor in some endeavor is to call it quits, for the sake of health and sanity. None of us can second-guess anyone else's need to make such decisions in the face of overwhelming injustice, discouragement, or pain.

You can respect your family's judgment, but you must still reserve the right to decide for yourself how much effort to invest in breaking barriers. Society does evolve, albeit erratically. You will have to cast your gaze widely—beyond your family—when you're looking for evidence that barriers can be broken. Over time, they *always* are.

Remember: Prejudice Is the Problem—Not You

When people in the mainstream view your family as different they don't mean it as a compliment. They mean you seem odd, threatening, unpredictable, or dangerous. But they act as though you—not their discomfort—are the problem. You have to reverse that equation and hang on to this truth: *Their prejudice is the problem.* It is the source of their discomfort and fear—not you.

You have the right to expect fair treatment based on your ability, not whether or not people with power are comfortable around you. Striving for fairness in a world of unthinking and unadmitted discrimination is a huge amount of work. It isn't fair that you should have to do it. But it's your only choice—except to give up.

Anger

Even when you see clearly that the problem of discrimination is not inside you but in society, that's likely to make you feel understandably angry, not only on your own behalf, but your family's. If your parents weren't able to grieve over their own losses and find ways to channel their anger over missed opportunities, you're likely to inherit these emotions.

If your parents' anger was muted or denied, you may wind up expressing it for them through acts of rebelliousness and defiance. Or, if your parents took their anger out on you in the form of criticism or harsh treatment, they may have prompted you to cut them off. We've seen the consequences of both of these strategies in **chapter 6:** they will keep you hobbled to the past.

Sort Out Your Own Grief and Anger from Your Family's

Your challenge is to sort out your own grief and anger from your family's. Yours you can do something about. You can mourn lost opportunities and heal the wounds that stem from prejudicial treatment. You can move beyond rebellion to the freedom of determining your own goals and moving forward with your own life. Theirs you can neither solve nor eliminate, although you can offer understanding and compassion, which in themselves are profoundly healing gifts.

IF YOU'VE BEEN CHOSEN TO BREAK BARRIERS

Your family may believe that the educational and economic barriers that held them back in the past are temporary. They believe tenacity and effort will enable succeeding generations to break through to new levels of financial rewards and social acceptance. These beliefs nurture hope and determination. Strengthened by such optimism, family members offer one another financial support and emotional encouragement for studying hard and finding good jobs.

As the Three Musketeers proclaim, *"All for one, and one for all."* If your family chose you to be the first to go to college, join a profession, earn a graduate degree, or make a fortune, then you've inherited a double-edged duty. On the one hand, everybody supports you. On the other hand, everybody knows exactly what you "owe" the family in exchange for their support.

Generational Conflicts

The harder you work at becoming well educated and successful in your career, the more you are exposed to a culture that values independence, freedom, self-expression, and individual fulfillment more than family loyalty and duty. The further you advance in your career, the farther you may have to travel—literally and figuratively—from your extended family. Over time, you may discover that what your family thinks you owe them bears little resemblance to your own interests, values, and goals.

These conflicts aren't anyone's fault. Generations have always clashed along the fault lines of social change. Each generation hopes their children will find greater success and acceptance than they did. But they also hope that success won't change the family's values and traditions. Yet education and careers do change people—how could they not? Being told this expectation is unrealistic, however, doesn't stop parents from feeling betrayed when they see their children acting in ways that amaze, shock, or scandalize them. Nor does it stop their children from feeling hurt that their parents don't understand that they live in a different world, where it is the future they must prepare for, not the past. And they must live their own lives.

You Live in the Present, Not Your Parents' Past

Indeed, you must live your own life. You don't have a choice. You live in the present world, not the one your parents remember and long to re-create. If you can accept that necessity without guilt, you can make your own career decisions—even if you depart from what your family feels you owe them—without having to shut your parents out of your life.

You can accept their amazement, dismay, even their disapproval, without feeling compelled to change either yourself or their attitudes. If so, you stand a much better chance than your parents did of avoiding feeling shocked, amazed, or scandalized by the changes your own children will make to adjust to the world you asked them to learn about and succeed within. Their success *will* change them, and it will do so in ways neither you nor they can now imagine. Be prepared.

Where Do You Fit In?

If you become the first in your family to earn a Ph.D., become a doctor, a scientist, or a company president, you may find that you have become less different from the rest of the world, but more so from the people who raised you, supported you, and invited you to achieve these things. They may not know what to make of you. And you may not know how to talk to them. Not only do you not fit in with outsiders, you may feel you don't fit in anywhere.

At family gatherings, you may elicit pride. But, whether you want to or not, you also bring hints of the outside world—through manners, speech, dress, vocabulary, and so forth—the world that discriminated against your family and caused them pain. They may assume that you now see them with the critical, condescending eyes of an outsider. They may accuse you of putting on airs, acting snobbish, or forgetting where you came from. Or they may act awkwardly around you and withdraw. The very success you were encouraged to attain has turned you into a reminder of your family's past disappointments, resentments, and wounds.

Your family members were focused on creating the opportunity for you to succeed. They didn't think about what would happen once you did. That's the problem. They didn't think that far ahead. Most people don't. But once you have succeeded and their feelings of loss and anger hit them, that may be all they can think about. They won't be able to see you—or how their hostility and resentment affect you—through the fog of their own dismay.

The Person to Fit In with Is Yourself

If you want to avoid resentment, then you need to make sure that the success you've achieved for your family is the same kind of success you want for yourself. If it is, then nothing family members say can rob you of your own pride and satisfaction in your achievement. If it isn't, then you need to leave behind your family's goals and find your own. The only person you absolutely have to fit in with, after all, is your own authentic self. And although it takes time, if you are doing work you love, you will find a community of others who are all "different" in the same way: they share your passion for their work.

Self-Acceptance

You have the right to act and speak naturally around your family. You don't owe it to anyone, anywhere, anytime, to downplay or disguise your achievements or your education in order to soothe someone else's insecurities. The cure for insecurity is self-acceptance, not avoiding people who trigger it. Pretending to be less educated or otherwise different than you are can't help your family. But it will hurt you. Remember, *you* are not the problem; their discomfort is. And it is their job to solve it. You can empathize with their struggle, but you can't go through it for them. Your own is challenging enough.

10

Abuse and Its Impact on Career or Job Choice

If you were abused as a child, you understand better than anyone else how it affected the way you feel and think about yourself. Clarifying how abuse has influenced your career path is an essential step in becoming free of its impact. If you weren't abused as a child, you almost certainly have friends and colleagues who were. Understanding the challenges they encounter—and how these are similar to or different from your own—can help you to bring greater insight and compassion to your friends and co-workers.

To assess the impact of abuse on your career, see **Exercise 16-4.**

MOVING FROM REENACTING THE PAST TO REINVENTING IT

Have you ever discovered yourself in a situation at work that felt uncannily similar to the type of abuse you experienced as a child?—a manager who disciplines harshly and unfairly in a tone of voice similar to that of a harsh, punitive parent? a supervisor whose inappropriate sexual advances bring back memories of a father, uncle, or cousin who sexually abused you when you were young? If so, the feelings these events brought back are likely to be profoundly familiar, too: defenselessness, vulnerability, anger, confusion, and betrayal.

Perhaps the similarity is built in to the work environment. For example, emergency medical technicians, crisis counselors, and health care workers in trauma centers are exposed every day to a constant flow of adrenaline and aftereffects of violence that may be familiar to them from growing up in chaotic, violent homes. Similarly, military personnel live with authoritarian structures and strict physical discipline that may duplicate their family upbringing. Not everyone makes these career choices because they were abused. But those who were may be drawn to such environments because they understand and feel at home in them.

Reliving relationships or events from childhood in the workplace is a common experience of abuse survivors. You didn't intend to. You don't want to. Nonetheless, it happens. Sometimes repeatedly. The cast changes, but the plot remains the same. Of course, everybody reenacts the past in his or her present life to some degree, but for abuse survivors, the stakes are higher. The danger is greater. The emotions are more extreme. The task of escaping or stopping the hurtful behavior can be more challenging.

The Distorting Lens of "Familiarity"

When we're children, home is the world. It defines what's real and true. The treatment we receive from our families teaches us what to expect from others later in life, especially those with power. If you grew up being harshly treated at home, harsh treatment on the job will seem literally familiar. You will see it through the distorting lens of your early experience. Mistreatment on the job may seem so predictable and normal that it is hard to see there is a problem, much less solve it. After all, how do you solve something that's inevitable?

The Stories of Virginia and Martin

Over her decade of work as a contract administrator Virginia had a half-dozen jobs. In each, her boss verbally abused her in ways that echoed the treatment she received from her alcoholic father. It was hard for her to see the pattern of abuse clearly, because she always assumed that being yelled at and insulted was the best anyone could expect from a boss. And she assumed that these tirades were her fault. Her first response to being yelled at was to try harder, just as she had tried harder, to no avail, to please her father.

Similarly, Martin, an aerospace engineer, works for a multinational corporation known for relentlessly driving employees to work harder. His employer maintains employee loyalty by constantly threatening layoffs and justifies these policies as essential to maximum profitability for shareholders.

Martin's parents started charging him rent when he was fourteen and got his first job. Martin liked working, because it got him away from his parents' continual demands that he clean the house, run errands, cook meals, and shop for groceries. They never thanked him for the work he did. Instead, they criticized him frequently. They were fond of pointing out that Martin was fortunate they provided him with shelter and food, and that unlike other parents they "hardly ever" hit him.

Martin feels overworked and underappreciated by his employer, but he, like Virginia, assumes that all employers exploit their employees. Looking for a better situation seemed pointless and reckless because employers are "all alike, they'll squeeze you dry. But you have to make a living, so they've got the upper hand."

Maybe It'll Be Different This Time

Because they don't expect fair or decent treatment from employers, abuse survivors work diligently for people who exploit or mistreat them. As children and adults, they keep striving for fairness and appreciation from people who are incapable of either response, because they haven't understood fully that it's not their fault—the defect is in the abusers, not themselves.

Virginia, for example, found that even when she got fed up enough with an abusive boss to quit, she felt strangely guilty, as though she were "abandoning" her boss. She even worried about how he would get along without her. She learned to feel guilty for things that weren't her fault early in life. Her father had become an alcoholic after his wife died, when both were in their early thirties. He felt bitter and overwhelmed.

Although Virginia and her siblings were devastated by their mother's death, her father acted as though it was his children's job to make up the loss to him by behaving perfectly. Whenever they misbehaved even slightly, they were harshly punished. No matter how hard his children tried to "make up" for their mother's death by behaving well, their father's grief continued, as did his anger and dissatisfaction with his children.

Virginia hoped that each new boss would be different and that someone would finally be satisfied with her hard work. Instead, they all turned out to be exactly like her father, never satisfied, always needy, and relentlessly ungrateful.

Martin, too, never stopped trying to please his parents. He hoped that someday he would stumble upon an achievement that would win him words of praise and the feeling that he "was good enough." The only approval Martin ever received from his parents was the "gift"—as they saw it—of being able to continue helping them, just as his current employer expects everything from him in exchange for the opportunity to continue giving them his all.

The Distorting Lens of Mistrust

Some people who were abused see through another kind of distorting lens. Rather than finding familiarity in a workplace that is harmful, they see danger and malevolence in situations that are neutral at worst or benign at best. When your trust has been betrayed early on by those you ought to be able to trust above all, you may approach all relationships with vigilance. No one may seem trustworthy. Wariness, however, may leave you feeling isolated and misunderstood, and can create difficulties in the exchange of favors and social banter that grease the wheels of most business relationships.

The Story of Candace

Candace, a junior accountant in a large firm, wanted to move up, but found herself blocked in promotions by her inability to network with colleagues. She froze up at her firm's corporate etiquette of quid pro quo—the exchange of professional favors for raises and promotions. She had chosen accounting as a profession because she hoped her work would be impersonal. Skill in statistics, rather than schmoozing, would enable her to succeed. Unfortunately, she discovered that politics were as important to her success at an accounting firm as they would be in any other industry.

As a child, Candace had been sexually abused by her uncle, who always tried to bribe her with favors for not "telling" on him. As a consequence, Candace now becomes angry and suspicious when anyone asks her for a favor. She avoids asking others for favors because she doesn't want to be indebted to anyone. Instinctively, she recoils from informal social contacts, fearing that others are ingratiating themselves only to gain power over her.

Although Candace's strongest emotions around her colleagues are fear and vulnerability, she knows that others perceive her as distant and aloof. Colleagues withdraw from her, and opportunities are awarded to co-workers who are more effective in playing office politics. Candace began her career determined that she would never allow herself to be exploited at work. Painfully, Candace now finds herself feeling at work much as she did as a child—isolated, fearful, and unsure whether there is anyone who deserves to be trusted.

How to Stop Repeating the Past

If you've found yourself, like Virginia, Martin, and Candace, reenacting painful scenarios from the past in your present work, then you no doubt share their frustration. You've probably wondered why you would do this to yourself. Haven't you been hurt enough already? Why seek more?

It's true that you are repeating the past. It's true that you've been hurt enough. But it isn't true that you are seeking to be abused again. What you are seeking, in fact, is the chance to correct your vision: to see abusive behavior clearly and to learn to prevent, escape, or stop it. In other words, the cast of characters may be the same, and the plot may feel similar, but the outcome doesn't have to be. The point of repeating the past is not to duplicate it, but to reinvent it.

Samskaras: Psychic Scars

The Hindu concept of *samskaras* provides a helpful metaphor for understanding what draws you to reenact the past. As Jungian analyst Roger Woolger has described them, *samskaras* are the karmic residue that past lives leave behind in our minds, a "psychic scar tissue" or "furrow in the psyche" that acts on our minds much the way a scratch on a phonograph record repeatedly pulls the needle back into the same groove.

Think of your childhood as your past life, and think of *karma* as the learning you must achieve to heal the psychic scars of abuse. Only then can the phonograph needle of your destiny move forward to the next groove. You are drawn to experiences and relationships that recapitulate past dangers and hurts not because you want to be, not because you enjoy them, but because your psychic and spiritual development requires it.

Moving Forward in Time

Reinventing your past is hard work, but it is possible. It is also necessary if you want to move forward from the groove in time you've gotten stuck repeating. You have to revisit the past—knowingly—in order to escape it's choke hold. Thomas Wolfe titled his best-known novel *You Can't Go Home Again.* But it isn't true. The truth is that home follows you everywhere you go. It's only when you recognize that fact that you can begin to leave home at all.

Absolve Yourself of Blame

First, you must absolve yourself of blame for the abuse—both in the past and in the present. It was never your fault. There was never anything you could do to fix or heal those who abused you. They didn't abuse you because there was anything wrong with you—but with them. Just as you were never responsible for abusive behavior in the past, you are not currently responsible for exploitative, unfair, or harsh treatment from any boss, colleague, or employer.

Choose Jobs and Employers Carefully

Recognize that the past isn't repeating itself on its own—your low expectations of the present have trapped you in it. All bosses aren't terrible. All employers aren't exploitative. The ones who are don't deserve to have you. You owe it to yourself to choose jobs and employers carefully. Use your past experiences to clarify the warning signals of potentially abusive employers, and steer clear of them at all costs.

Develop Criteria for Loyalty and Trust

Develop specific and stringent criteria for people and organizations you feel loyal to and trust. Loyalty isn't something you automatically owe any person or organization until they have earned it, through fair, caring, and respectful treatment. Don't trust people unless they meet your criteria, but don't mistrust everyone without cause. Getting rid of distorting lenses means seeing individuals as they actually are, not as others in the past have led you to assume everyone will be.

PROTECTOR, HEALER, OR ENFORCER OF JUSTICE

People who have been neglected or mistreated as children sometimes dedicate their lives to preventing others from being abused, to helping victims, or to bringing justice and/or rehabilitation to offenders. Working in law enforcement, protective services, social work, counseling, education, or health care provides some survivors a means of redressing their own abuse by fulfilling the roles of protector, healer, or enforcer of justice. Within these roles, they find a sense of power, effectiveness, vindication, and freedom of expression that was denied them as children.

If you've invested your hard-won knowledge of the devastating impact of child abuse into the fight against it, then you know firsthand how emotionally challenging such work is. Not just because you are exposed constantly to reminders of your own pain, but also because the fight can be all-consuming. As happens for many, your greatest risk may be that you fight so hard you become a casualty of the struggle.

You Can't Rescue Everyone

You may feel tempted to rescue all suffering children singlehandedly, or to bring all perpetrators to justice. With such temptations come the hazards of burnout, of blurring boundaries between your personal and professional lives, and of caring so much for others that you forget to take proper care of yourself. Your physical and emotional health, and your family and friendships may suffer.

Watch for Warning Signs

You have to be able to draw effective boundaries between your work and your personal life, between the needs of those you want to protect and your own. If you can't, your work may appear to redress abuse, but on the inside you may actually be *reenacting* it. Warning signs include putting in long hours without adequate rest and vacation time; taking on more responsibility for saving or healing others than is possible or realistic; feeling guilty or unworthy when you aren't actively engaged in "the fight."

If you struggle to set effective limits on your work, it's important to ask yourself where and how you learned to take advantage of yourself. In your heart, do you believe that you deserve respect, nourishment, and care? Or do you believe that your worth derives from how much care you take of others?

Be Careful with Yourself

Beneath compassion and a desire to protect others, you may still feel shame and grief in response to your own past. You need to heal these painful feelings first in order for your work truly to redress abuse rather than subtly reenact it. Most abuse survivors I have known possess enormous resiliency. But many also struggle to remember that they deserve to invest as much or more energy into taking care of themselves as they do for other people—and that they must do so every day. Preventing damage to yourself is just as important as preventing damage to others. The former is *your* primary responsibility; the latter you share with many others. *Self-neglect* is the Achilles' heel of abuse survivors. Be careful with yourself.

STOP WORKING TOO HARD AND ENJOYING TOO LITTLE

Overwork and perfectionism may appear to be virtues. To the extent they enable you to attain status and wealth, these qualities may be admired and envied by other people. But there's a difference between *choosing* to work hard because you enjoy it, and feeling compelled to work hard because you're afraid to stop. The former springs from desire. The latter will keep you too busy to find out what your desires really are.

If your family was chaotic, violent, or disorganized when you were growing up, you may feel driven as an adult to get things under control and keep them there. Achievement, perfectionism, and workaholism can become ends in themselves. If so, work provides not enjoyment, but a clear, safe focus for your mind. You may, in fact, feel anxious and apprehensive anytime you are *not* working. If you aren't busy keeping things organized, chaos might erupt. After all, it did when you were younger.

Fran's Story

If you began working hard as a child to take care of your family, then it may never have occurred to you that work is something you choose, much less choose based on your own interest and enjoyment. Fran, at thirty-eight, is the youngest-ever president of a chain of retail stores. She began working for the company immediately after graduation from college, not because it was what she always wanted to do, but because she needed the job to pay off college loans. She then earned an MBA at night and steadily advanced. She rarely takes vacations because the company's needs come first. Besides, she worries about what could go wrong when she's not there.

Fran grew up as the oldest child in a home with alcoholic parents. The environment was chaotic, with lots of fighting—hitting as well as yelling. Her mother relied upon her to take care of the younger children and to retrieve her father from his favorite bar. Her father relied upon her to act as peacemaker between himself and his wife. He was always proud of her. "Thank God for Frannie," he would say.

Fran kept her family organized as she now keeps her company organized. If she slowed down, she'd have time to think and feel, which was the "last thing on earth" she wanted, then or now. When Fran was a child, no one in her family cared about what she wanted. They were too busy getting what they wanted from her. Now, as an adult, Fran focuses on working hard to stave off crises at work so that others will be proud and satisfied with her. As when she was growing up, she feels she can't stop taking charge, because "You're only as good as the latest crisis you've contained."

A Double Life

If you grew up being expected to keep your family stable and calm, then you may have learned to expect the impossible from yourself. Not only is it unfair to ask a child to handle family crises, it's impossible for anyone—of any age—to control others' behavior and emotions. If you continue expecting yourself to create safety and order for others, then no matter how hard you work or how successful others think you are, you're bound to feel like a failure. Not because you're inadequate, but because your standards are unrealistic.

Fran's success, for example, has not increased her confidence or enabled her to take pride in her achievement. In fact, all that success has changed for Fran is that she works harder and worries more. Although others envy her achievement, she feels she leads a double life. Outwardly, she has an impressive job title, financial rewards, and the promise of greater achievements in the future. Inwardly, she feels stressed and pressured, fearful of making mistakes, and anxious that disaster might strike at any moment—and take with it the illusion of her competence. She doesn't believe in her own success, because it hinges upon an impossible attainment: perfect stability and harmony. Neither Fran nor any other mere mortal can achieve this goal for any company, or for any family.

Take Time Out to Find the Real You

If you work all the time, strive for perfection, and stave off crises at work and at home, you may have attained what others perceive as the American Dream. But you may also feel stressed and tired, never confident that your success will last, or that you'll be able to stave off the next disaster looming just over the horizon. You may have fallen into this pressured way of life not because you wanted it, but because you knew no other way to live.

The only way out is the way that may scare you the most, because it runs counter to everything you see as your primary value in life: *stop working.* Rather, retire immediately from the job of hero, crisis manager, and overachiever. Join the ranks of fallible humans. It's all you ever really were, anyway. And it's all your family had the right to expect of you in the first place.

The Only Heroism That Counts

To feel successful on the inside, which is entirely different from looking successful on the outside, you need to take the time to explore your own emotions: how you felt about the way your family treated you, what you want now and in the future. No one ever bothered to ask what *you* wanted, but it's not too late for you to start looking. You will find the clues to who you really are as soon as you take time to look for them. When you succeed in finding out who you are and do your best to live in accord with that truth, you will find that it is the only kind of heroism that counts—or, indeed, is possible for anyone.

RECLAIMING GOALS AND OPPORTUNITIES

Abuse takes a heavy emotional toll on people. It can take years to fully comprehend the aftereffects, much less to heal them. If this was true for you, then you've probably invested much of your time and energy as an adult into reclaiming your emotional health and freedom, and you may have had less time and energy to invest in educational opportunities and career goals. Here's how to start shifting the balance.

You Can Get Rid of the Pain

Abusers steal from their victims the freedom to explore dreams, develop talents, take advantage of opportunities, and make independent plans by placing themselves, their own needs, their own rage and pain, in the center of the child's world. This is a terrible distortion of power and trust.

Ferreting out all the pain, shame, and rage from your life that the abuser left behind is a massive and time-consuming undertaking. The good news is that you can get rid of it, and you don't have to do it alone. Many types of psychotherapy, bodywork, pastoral counseling, and other forms of emotional healing can help you. But the challenging news is that the work of self-healing may have to come first, before you are free to explore new goals or reclaim old ones you deferred.

For more on finding a therapist, see **Appendix 1.**

You Deserve to Feel Proud

Typically, young adults spend their late teens and twenties, and sometimes a good portion of their thirties, experimenting with different careers. If your energies were diverted from career development into healing the emotional scars of abuse, then you may have watched your peers seemingly surpass you professionally and/or financially. Finding the strength and resiliency to survive and heal from abuse is an extraordinary achievement, but it's private. It isn't easily understood or widely celebrated. It is, however, still real. Even if only you and your therapist and a few loved ones ever fully understand your courage and tenacity, you deserve to feel proud of yourself.

Lessons That Surpass a Diploma

If you survived childhood abuse, then you have learned the kind of lessons about life and humanity—its frailties and strengths—that aren't taught in school, for which you'll never receive a degree. In the end, the legacy of wisdom and compassion and truth you can pass on far surpasses in value the attainment of diplomas, degrees, titles, and other tangible kinds of success. No doubt you want the other kind of success, too—the success that comes from finding satisfying work, and from earning your own livelihood. You can get there. Many others have.

Your Most Important Achievement

With patience and tenacity, you can work step by step toward having both kinds of success. Remember that your survival already demonstrates you have attained the most important achievement of all—becoming a strong, resilient human being who seeks truth, health, and wisdom.

OVERCOMING THE SPIRITUAL WOUNDS OF ABUSE

One of the most painful effects of childhood abuse is the spiritual havoc it wreaks. Children whose emotions and bodies have been violated by adults have witnessed the betrayal of a sacred moral trust—that the innocent and powerless will receive protection, care, and love from those who are older, stronger, and more powerful. If children can't rely upon adults to revere this bond, then how are they to grow up trusting in the sacredness of anything or anyone?

Searching for Hope and Faith in a Violent World

Everyone struggles to find hope and faith in a world fraught with deception, betrayal, cruelty, and danger. Trying to fathom the eternal tension between good and evil, war and peace, greed and generosity challenges us all. If you were abused, your encounter with betrayal and violence is not theory but personally experienced truth.

These spiritual wounds are just as devastating as physical or emotional wounds, because they shape your feelings about being human, about the world you live in, about the meaning not just of your own life but of life itself. You may have been left with a sense of the insignificance of individual desires for happiness in a world in which the powers that rule—be they parental, social, or divine—have demonstrated indifference to the suffering of innocent children, and to your own particular pain.

Don't Settle for Less

If you feel this way, you may be tempted to settle for a career path that feels adequate rather than one that touches your heart and expresses your dreams. Don't. Not only is it a loss for you if you settle for less than fully exploring your gifts, it's a loss for the world. Your vibrancy and vitality matter. It's important that you find out what you love to do and that you find a way to do it. Every person who does so expands the amount of love in the world and becomes an example to all others. You are significant.

If you didn't begin life with a belief in your own significance, you can and must invent and sustain it. Don't believe that you don't have specific talents and gifts. Everyone does, even if they are buried deep within you. You can find them. But you won't bother trying if you don't believe they matter. They do. A sense of significance isn't something you have to wait for. It isn't something someone else gives you. It's something you claim for yourself. And every time you do, your example makes it easier for others to claim theirs as well.

Rejecting Religion

Like many abuse survivors, you have probably struggled with the question: If God is all-knowing or all-powerful, why did God allow me to be abused? If the religious tradition you were brought up in didn't provide an answer that felt convincing and compelling to you, then you probably left religion behind.

Letting Go of Illusions: Dana's Story

Dana was raised in the Christian tradition. He was abused as a child by a "cantankerous patriarch" all too reminiscent of the god he encountered in Bible stories. Dana rejected the religion he was brought up in because he thought it "oversimplified" life. You can only believe in God, he decided, if you are willing to look at a slim portion of reality that excludes child abuse, or if you're willing to chalk everything up to "God's will." If the abuse he experienced in his youth was part of a "divine plan," then Dana didn't want anything to do with such a divinity.

Dana had stopped expecting fairness from his parents long ago. He decided that the only way he could come to terms with his parents' cruelty was to let go of illusions about what parents are "supposed" to be, and about human nature itself. Only by letting go of "all illusions" about people and God could he find the truth. But it was a challenging, gritty truth, which often left him feeling profoundly alone and deeply discouraged, devoid of spiritual sustenance. It also made him feel strong, as though every day he were swallowing a "bitter pill" that gave him the endurance to go to his job as counselor for emotionally troubled families, and "shore up" the chaos once again.

Rebuilding Faith

One way to heal such spiritual wounds is to seek different concepts of divinity than those provided by your family. For some, this quest leads to traditional Western religions that were absent or undernourished in their families. Others turn to non-Western or alternative theologies, such as Buddhism and other Eastern religions, feminist theology, goddess or neo-pagan rituals, twelve-step programs, or the eclectic blend called New Age spirituality.

Dana found that his work on the front lines of chaotic families led him over time to shed his view of God as a "being." He saw too many innocent people suffer. As he released his concept of a "personal" god who judges and then punishes or rewards human beings based on their behavior, he sought other definitions of divinity. As he did so, his anger at God began to fade.

Dana was drawn to the Native American idea of a Great Spirit that dwells within all life. The idea of a "circle of life" has helped him to regain a sense of community and a healing connection with nature. He also studied shamanistic beliefs and practices, in which healers are initiated into wisdom and skill by undergoing a rite of passage through spiritual dangers. Dana now views his own childhood as an initiation into human suffering, from which he has derived the skills of a healer.

Look for Beliefs That Sustain You

We all need beliefs that sustain us. If the abuse you experienced as a child has destroyed your confidence in the beliefs you grew up with, then you may have to actively search for others that are complex, clear-eyed, and tough-minded enough to encompass the truth of your experience of violence, betrayal, and injustice. Many others have sought faith and clarity before you, and chances are that you will be able to find something to sustain you, whether it is based on religion, philosophy, theology, meditation, mythology, or art.

But you won't find it if you don't look. And until you find it, you won't be able to integrate your work with your beliefs—because you won't be clear what they are; you'll only know what they are not. Letting go of illusions is only an intermediate step. The ultimate goal is to find out what you do believe, and then to work hard to express those beliefs in every part of life, including your career.

Part Three

WORK, SUCCESS, AND MONEY

✦

11

How Family Values Work For and Against Us

Every family conveys values and beliefs about work, success, and money. If your family's values mesh with your own, you can find strength and guidance in them throughout your career. If they don't, you have to follow your own. Otherwise you'll build a career that your parents take pride in, but that leaves you frustrated and empty. That sounds straightforward enough. But before you can follow your values, you have to figure out what they are—and whether they differ from those you were taught.

To clarify the values about work that you learned growing up, you have to ask not just what your parents *said* they valued, but what their everyday behavior *demonstrated* was important to them. Your parents may have told you they believed that money was less important than goodness and honesty, but if they argued constantly about money—not goodness or honesty—their *behavior* demonstrated they were conflicted about how important money should be.

You may wonder later in life how you learned to feel tense and conflicted about money, and why you're never sure how important it should be in career decisions. The answer is: your parents' behavior, not their words, was your most important teacher. As Albert Schweitzer said, "Example isn't the *main* thing in influencing others. It is the *only* thing."

To explore your family's values about work, success, and money, see **Exercise 16-3.**

QUESTIONS EVERY FAMILY ANSWERS ABOUT WORK, SUCCESS, AND MONEY

All families answer the three questions below. Everyday events communicate the answers clearly and persuasively to family members. As you read what follows, compare these answers with those you learned from your family.

- Why do we work?
- What does money mean?
- How do you know you're a success?

WHY DO WE WORK?

If your parents loved work, they probably saw its purpose as growth and creativity as well as livelihood, and integrated these purposes in their careers. Such people, however, are rare, not because we wouldn't all love to view work as noble and healthy, but because such an integration is difficult to achieve. Since Adam and Eve were banished from Eden, toil—underpaid, overworked, and without much choice—has been humanity's lot. Let's look at two more frequent answers about why we work: to be good and to do good for others, and to build and maintain security for your family.

To Be Good and Do Good for Others

This sounds like a noble purpose. And it certainly can be. But unless it includes the caveat "while also doing good for yourself," nobility can become oppressive. This answer may spring from religious convictions. Or it may stem from earlier generations' encounters with social injustice.

POWERFUL LESSONS HIDDEN IN ORDINARY MEMORIES

Margaret's parents were committed social activists whose own parents brought them up on stories of the poverty and discrimination they'd experienced when they first immigrated to the United States. Growing up, Margaret learned that the purpose of work was social change, not personal fulfillment. These don't have to be mutually exclusive goals. They become so when people pursue the former without regard for the latter—because they assume fulfillment is irrelevant to work. That's what Margaret did.

After a decade of performing demanding, meaningful work as a community organizer in impoverished urban neighborhoods, Margaret grew impatient and unhappy with the demands of her job. She was shocked at her "ignoble" and "selfish" dreams of finding work that would be "lighthearted and enjoyable—work that achieved something positive not just for others but for me, too."

It's the ordinariness of childhood memories that makes the lessons we derive from them seem like common sense rather than parental advice or rules. Margaret's parents never gave her a single word of career advice. But she vividly remembered an incident from the age of nine that crystallized the values that shaped her career.

She had begged her parents for a pair of red cowboy boots as a Christmas present. But on Christmas morning, she received a pair of sensible, black rubber snowboots instead. At first, she was angry at her parents for getting the wrong present. But as she watched her parents' faces—seeing they expected her to thank them—she understood that her parents hadn't made a mistake, they had given her a lesson. They had substituted what they thought Margaret *ought* to want for what she desired.

Margaret immediately felt guilty for having wanted such a frivolous present in the first place. She swallowed her disappointment, smiled, and thanked her parents for the snowboots. In retrospect, she feels that she has been smiling and saying thank you for what she didn't want, but thought she should, ever since. But the habit went so far back, and seemed so routine and necessary, that it took years for her to figure out its impact on her career.

Why It's Important to Know What You Want

If you learned as a child to judge your desires—some were worthy, some were not—then you probably brought the same moral stance to career decisions. Your career equivalents to Margaret's red boots may seem frivolous and unworthy of a responsible person. Over time, you may have stopped being aware of what your desires really were, because they seemed irrelevant to a "serious" career.

Desires, however, aren't morally good or bad in themselves. It's what we do in response to desires that can be good or bad. The only way to know yourself fully is to find out what you really want—even if it's "frivolous" or "selfish." You have to stop judging your desires and instead learn from them who you really are. You might not choose to follow every desire. But you must do the choosing.

You're the only one who can discover the right mix of frivolity and seriousness, selfishness and generosity you need in order to be happy. The mix you choose can be different from your parents', but you can be an equally worthwhile human being. Even Emma Goldman said, "If I can't dance, I don't want to be part of your revolution."

To Build and Maintain Security for Your Family

For many people, work means getting a job. It's something everybody has to do. It's great if you find one you like, but it's more important that it be secure. Fulfillment is something you find with your family and friends in your spare time. And perhaps, if you've planned ahead, in your retirement. This attitude toward work is so common and so practical, it might seem to brook no debate. But it is a *belief* about work, not a *fact.* It's rooted in family histories of economic hardships, such as layoffs, bankruptcies, or other financial shocks.

OFF TO THE SALT MINES

David grew up in a middle-class family. When he graduated from college with a liberal arts degree, he applied to a state agency for an administrative position. It was a chance to "get his foot in the door" and work his way up the career ladder, as his father had done before him. David found his work neither pleasurable nor miserable. He never expected work to be more than a necessary burden. Although David and his parents had been financially secure, his grandparents had struggled to make ends meet working in factories. To them, having a white-collar job—*any* white-collar job—was a luxury.

David's first impression of work was formed as a child when his father would pause by the kitchen door before leaving for work, smiling wryly, to say, "Off to the salt mines, kids. Enjoy your youth." Every Friday, David's father continued his "retirement countdown," crossing off another week on the calendar and announcing the remaining years, months, and days until he was free of his employer's "ball and chain." From his father's behavior, David learned that work was drudgery, which a mature and responsible person accepted with forbearance, grateful for the security of a paycheck.

David vowed in high school that he would never be like his father—he would find a passion in life. But no burning passion arose. When he graduated from college, he felt aimless and confused. Without intending to, but without knowing how to resist, he was drawn to repeat his father's path. He figured that someday he would get married and have a family, and would value the security of a civil service position. He had no other image of work than that of his father, heading off for the "salt mines." Like his father, David took pleasure not in his work but in the satisfaction of doing his duty as a breadwinner.

Transforming Security from a Primary Goal into a By-product of Working

If you grew up with parents who viewed work as a necessary burden, your challenge is to transform security into a by-product of working, not its primary goal. Doing so is no dishonor to your parents. To the contrary, your freedom to redefine the purpose of work honors the support they gave you. It's also the greatest gift you can pass on to your children. (For more on helping your children, see **chapter 21.**)

WHAT DOES MONEY MEAN?

Money is like food. We all need it to live. But we vary wildly in our definition of need and in the emotional meanings we assign to it. Career decisions are always intertwined with money. To make effective decisions, therefore, we have to understand what money means. What did we grow up thinking money would do for us, or reveal about us?

"Enough" Money Gives You Abundance and Happiness

"The rich are different from you and I," wrote Fitzgerald in *The Great Gatsby.* If you want to know how your family viewed money, ask yourself how they defined the "difference." Money exerts power over us because of what we imagine our lives could become if we ever had enough. The problem is that "enough" is subjective. It's a state of mind, not a number. You can't purchase a feeling of abundance. Nor can money set you free from feelings of scarcity. These truths are timeless and obvious—yet they are also as hard to hang on to as a bar of wet soap.

WHAT IS "ENOUGH"?

Abby works as an office manager for a university. Her husband works as an accountant. Their combined income enables them to live in a four-bedroom suburban house, drive two cars, and take one family vacation every year. She enjoys her job and likes her co-workers, but feels she ought to look for a better-paying job so she can afford her dream house, send her children to private colleges, and travel not just to Florida, but to Europe and Asia.

One day a new clerk complained to Abby that she couldn't possibly understand his need for a higher salary because she was "rich." Abby was shocked. She never felt that her family had "enough." But from the clerk's point of view she had not just enough, she lived in luxury. He felt about her, she realized, the same way she felt about upper-level administrators at the university. To her, their lives seemed privileged. Yet, she guessed, they probably felt they didn't have enough compared to corporate executives. If you're preoccupied with what you don't have, you'll be perpetually dissatisfied with what you do have.

FINDING ABUNDANCE WITHIN

If you grew up longing for enough money to give you a feeling of abundance, you need to reexamine this assumption. No matter how much money you earn, somebody else will have more. If you focus on what you can't afford—and there will always be things you can't afford—you will always feel deprived. Unless you know how to feel free and abundant on the inside, having enough will constantly elude you, no matter how much you buy.

Two shifts in attitude can help you find abundance within:

- **First,** work on valuing everything you have that you can't purchase with money, such as friendships, character, and knowledge. If you have these things, you truly have abundance. If you don't have them, money will never substitute for them.
- **Second,** assess everything you already own. How much do you really need? How much is a luxury? In this country, most of us are surrounded by luxuries we take for granted, from cars to CDs to the time we spend watching television. Balance the time you spend imagining what it would be like to have more with time spent imagining how your life looks to those who have less.

Money Is How You Keep Score

If you think of salaries as a measure of self-esteem, then the higher your income, the more valuable you are as a person—money is a way to keep score of your worth. This point of view isn't just common, it's built into our economy. The more an organization needs your services, the more they'll pay you. The more interchangeable your skills are with those of others, the less they will pay you. Your work may be important and valuable, but if your employer believes they can easily find others to do it, the laws of supply and demand will dictate a lower salary. The people with the most money, therefore, are entitled to the highest self-esteem. Aren't they?

Identify the Game You Are Scoring

First, you have to understand which game you're scoring. If you've earned the most money, do you win at life, or something smaller?

Brad grew up wearing designer clothes, attending private schools, and owning the most expensive toys. "You deserve the best," his parents told him. By implication, having less than the "best" meant that was all you deserved. Brad's career decisions were driven by the need to prove his worth by being able to afford the "best." Earning a high salary meant he was proving his worth. Money was self-esteem. And being envied by friends for his material possessions was equivalent in Brad's mind to receiving their esteem, as well.

The limitations of keeping score with money became clear to Brad later in life, when he woke up one day and realized he was surrounded by magnificent "stuff," but hated his life. He had overdeveloped skills at earning money and underdeveloped skills at everything else. It finally dawned on him that the game you win with money is played on a narrow field—on which money overrules curiosity, creativity, or pleasure. Yet he was afraid to find a more expansive playing field because he thought he would look like a loser to his parents, himself, and his friends—to everyone who was still "keeping score."

Define What You Will Win and What You Won't

If you use money as a means of keeping score, it's important to understand the limits of what you win, and what you won't win.

You'll win points for proving you can buy the best. But you'll only win them with people who are scoring the same game. No one else will believe that material possessions prove anything about your worth as a human being.

You'll win the envy of many people. But envy is not the same as esteem—in fact, envy distances people rather than draws them closer to you. It is not the same as fondness or admiration.

You'll win more opportunities to play the game and score more points. But you may find it increasingly hard to leave the game behind. Even if you hate what you're doing, you'll find it hard to risk losing money by trying something new and different that you might enjoy more.

FIND WHAT IS WORTHY IN YOUR OWN EXPERIENCE

Realistically, it's hard not to use money to keep score. You do it whenever you negotiate a salary or set a fee. But you can be clear in your own mind about the narrowness of what money measures. It measures your luck and skill in making money. That's all. It tells you nothing about human worth or what you deserve. For that, you have to seek alternate measures, based not on sums but on qualities such as compassion, commitment, vitality, and creativity. Better yet, since qualities are difficult to quantify, abandon the quest for measurement altogether. Forget about comparing your worth to that of others. Focus instead on finding what is *worthy in your own experience.*

Bribery

In many families, money is openly used as a both a carrot and a stick. Your parents may have offered to pay tuition, but only for the college of their choice. They'll buy you a car, but only if you choose a model they like. The manipulation is usually obvious to all, but transparency doesn't diminish its effectiveness.

WHY BRIBERY IS BOTH EFFECTIVE AND DESTRUCTIVE

Bribes encourage financial dependence and foster fear and self-doubt. Throughout her childhood Alice's parents would lavish presents on her as long as she was "good"—which meant she let them choose her friends, her clothes, and her private school. Of course, her parents said they wanted to ensure Alice did "what was best for her" because they loved her.

Alice always understood her parents manipulated her with money. She knew their love was conditioned by her obedience.

After she grew up, her parents subsidized a lifestyle she'd never have been able to afford on her salary as a freelance writer. Whenever Alice defied their wishes, her parents would threaten to cut her out of their will. Alice would then comply. Not only had she developed a taste for "nice things," but she feared that being cut out of her parents' will would render her years of catering to them meaningless. She would truly be left with nothing.

Alice reached a turning point when she won a year-long fellowship to a writers colony in a distant state. Her parents told her that if she "abandoned" them for a year, she would lose her inheritance. Alice had to calculate what was at stake. She knew that if she took the fellowship, her parents would accuse her of not loving them and not appreciating everything they had given her. But she also knew she would gain freedom, confidence, and self-respect. Ultimately, Alice decided these gains outweighed the losses. She took the fellowship and discovered to her surprise that what she felt more than anything else—more than guilt or fear or anger—was relief.

Being True to Yourself Is a Necessity

If your parents used money to bribe you into obedience and encouraged you to define loving them as letting them have their way, then you must separate the meanings of money, obedience, and love. None of these belong together. You deserve to be loved for who you are, not for the person your parents pay you to pretend to be. Your love for yourself requires that you follow your truth—even when it means defying your parents' wishes.

Being true to yourself does not mean you do not love your parents, or that you don't appreciate what they've given you in the past. It *does* mean that you refuse to be bullied or bribed into submission in exchange for "love." Such a refusal takes courage and staying power, but brings relief, freedom, and belief in yourself. You're likely to discover that the more often you choose yourself, the easier the choice becomes. Eventually, you won't see it as a choice, but as a necessity. At that point, it will be. You will have lost your fear. No one will ever again be able to convince you that love and obedience—enforced with money—are the same.

HOW DO YOU KNOW YOU'RE A SUCCESS?

Success is a concept we define in inner and outer ways. The inner ways have to do with feeling proud of ourselves and satisfied with our lives. The outer ways have to do with external signs of power, prestige, and achievement, such as job titles, salary, and material possessions. If your family encouraged you to believe that attaining the external signs of success would produce the inner feelings of pride and satisfaction, you may feel shocked or dismayed when you discover they don't always do so. You can use the shock, however, to explore the distinction between inner and outer success and to create your own definitions of each.

You're a Success When You're at the Top of the "Career Ladder"

Climbing to the top of the career ladder is a popular and influential metaphor for success. It developed in conjunction with large, bureaucratic, hierarchical, pyramid-shaped organizations. Climbing the ladder means striving for higher job titles, a greater span of control over employees who report to you, and of course, larger salaries. By the terms of the metaphor, you are more successful than people lower than you on the ladder, and less successful than those above you. Position is everything.

The Only Direction That Leads to Success Is Up

Sandy's parents encouraged her to aim for the top. Both of them had attained vice president status within large corporations before they retired. They never introduced themselves as "former marketing specialists" or "former insurance executives." It was always "former vice presidents." To them, the industry you worked in—even your functional area—didn't matter. They believed all career decisions should be guided by pursuit of the highest possible rank.

Her parents were shocked when Sandy accepted a lateral transfer in order to work on a marketing project that interested her. In their minds, being "stuck" on the same "rung" was equivalent to failure; it meant she was going nowhere in her career.

Sandy, however, cared more about what she learned from work than about her rank. She chose projects based on the skills she wanted to develop. The organizations she worked for were shaped differently from the pyramids her parents had climbed. They were flatter, and required lateral movement from one team-based project to another. And in these days of mergers and downsizing, Sandy found that organizations changed shape so often, you couldn't lay a ladder against one long enough to climb up it. In fact, you were likely to fall off trying.

The Limits of the Ladder

If your family encouraged you to measure success according to your position on the career ladder, you may want to review the limitations of this metaphor. The ladder skews career decisions toward jobs with chances for advancement. It reinforces ambition for upward mobility and neglects interest and enjoyment. It also ignores the value of learning and the quality or substance of work. If you're the president of an organization, you're successful no matter how silly or harmful your company's product is. By contrast, if you save lives or create peace, but your rank is "low," you're not a success. Does this make sense?

You're a Success When You've Gotten Exactly What You Wanted

Call it the "bootstrap" philosophy. If you work hard and you're smart, you'll succeed in getting exactly what you want. If you don't get it, you've failed. You didn't work hard enough. You weren't smart enough. Your work wasn't good enough. You must have done something wrong. The belief that hard work will be rewarded with success is as comforting as the belief that failure must have been earned is disturbing. These are common but painful, profoundly unrealistic assumptions.

Unforeseen and uncontrollable circumstances—that have little to do with effort or merit—play a much greater role in whether or not we get what we want than we may care to admit. If you doubt it, try this simple exercise: On one side of a sheet of paper, list everything that you *cannot control.* On the other side, list everything you are sure you *can control.* You are likely to find a long and far-ranging list of things you can't control: weather, bosses, your children, the economy, other people's opinions, your own emotions, your dog's behavior, and so on. Your list of everything you can control will probably have one item: how you respond to all the things you can't control.

Fear of Failure Leads to Avoiding Risks

Did your parents praise you extravagantly when you got good grades or won at spelling bees, track meets, or softball games?

When you or your team lost or you got less than an A, did they berate you for not trying hard enough or for failing? The implication was that success was within your grasp, and that failure was your fault. If you didn't succeed in attaining your parents' standards, you must have done something wrong.

If you grew up believing that failing meant you had done something wrong, you may have learned to avoid taking risks. Did you major in college in a subject you loved, or one you knew you could excel in? Have you always looked for jobs you were sure you already knew perfectly—to the point of boredom—instead of ones where you might flounder, make mistakes, but also learn something new? The consequence of avoiding risks is that you may succeed—at things you don't care about.

If You Want to Learn, You Have to Embrace Mistakes

If you grew up defining success as getting what you want, then you may try only for things you're sure you can get. Or if you try new things, you may berate yourself if you don't perform perfectly the first and every subsequent time. You must have done something wrong, because you control your destiny. Right?

Wrong. You can't control destiny. You can only discover it unfolding around you. No one gets everything right all the time. No one gets everything he or she wants. Being smart and successful doesn't mean you never make mistakes, it means you work hard at learning from the ones you're bound to make. The larger the mistake, the more you'll have to learn. If you want to learn new things, you have to embrace mistakes.

If you want to develop compassion for yourself and others, you have to recognize how much of life is determined by currents and eddies we do not anticipate and cannot control. That doesn't mean you shouldn't try. But it does mean that you cannot hold yourself accountable for circumstances beyond your control. It also means that you can't define success as getting exactly what you want.

A DEFINITION OF SUCCESS THAT NURTURES LEARNING

If you want a definition of success that nurtures learning, here are questions to ask about your work:

- Are you learning what you want?
- Are you challenged by your work?
- Do you enjoy your work?
- Does your work contribute something useful to others?
- At the end of the day, do you feel proud of what you've done?

If you answer yes to all of these, then you're succeeding beautifully at something more important than climbing the career ladder. You're leading an interesting and productive life. This achievement will give you pride and pleasure all your life, and earn you no title whatsoever—except perhaps that of being wise.

This definition of success equips you to fearlessly pursue the new, the untried, the inviting. Life becomes an adventure, rather than a performance. You may not get exactly what you wanted, but you'll probably learn a tremendous amount from whatever it is you find along the way.

12

Overcoming Beliefs That Block Change and Personal Success

You may discover differences between your family's values about work, success, and money and your own. If so, you'll have to adjust the work you do or the way you do it to align these with your values. As you undertake this challenge, you will encounter another set of values you learned from your family—those about the benefits and dangers of *change*.

People often assume that once they know how they want to change, the hardest work is behind them. The clarity of their goals will act like gravity, and they will coast downhill toward desired changes. It's unsettling to discover that, to the contrary, when you're at risk of actually getting closer to your goals, inner barriers kick up more stubbornly than ever before—fears, doubts, cynicism, hopelessness, or feelings of futility.

Don't be caught off guard if instead of coasting toward your goals, you are initially held back by fear of change and doubts about your ability to succeed. These feelings are usually rooted in unexamined, inherited beliefs about change that you can clarify, challenge, and modify. This chapter describes some common barriers to change, and suggests shifts in attitude to help you overcome them. As you read, compare your own beliefs about change with the following statements.

"I SHOULD BE ABLE TO CHANGE COMPLETELY OVERNIGHT"

Do you envision change as a straight line linking one stage in your life to another? Once you decide to change, you should just do it. No backsliding, no stumbling, no self-doubt. Not only is this attitude unrealistic, it sets you up to fail. If you can't change your life instantly and completely—and no one can—you may prematurely decide your efforts are pointless, and give up.

If you hold this belief about change, you probably grew up in a family that rewarded you for results, not for trying hard or for enjoying what you were doing. If your parents were impatient with you, you may have learned to be impatient with yourself. Perfectionist standards may cause you to view failure as shameful. Instead of giving yourself adequate time to work steadily toward your goals, you may get bogged down in self-criticism, or you may view change as too risky, and never try.

Change Is a Spiral Path

Change isn't linear. No one bounds steadily forward toward his or her goals without a backward glance or a stumble. In fact, backward glances and stumbles serve three important purposes:

1. They ensure that we do not change too quickly—that we're truly *ready* for change.
2. They force us to keep recommitting to our goals, so we're sure we still *want* them.
3. They give us a sense of *continuity* between the person we are becoming and the person we used to be.

Only on a map is a straight line the shortest distance between two points. In life, the shortest distance between one place and another is the rhythmic looping motion of the spiral. Thinking of change as a spiral enables you to value delays and false starts in your journey as well as successes. When you loop backward over familiar territory, you aren't reversing direction. You're continuing your journey by moving on to the next loop of the spiral. If you make a mistake, repeat a bad habit, fall into an old fear—these are opportunities to relearn important lessons. A slow, steady pace is benevolent and necessary, not a symptom of laziness or failure.

"I SHOULDN'T CHANGE IF I WILL HURT MY FAMILY"

Are you your family's keeper? Is it ethical to pursue changes that may disappoint or upset people you love? If you grew up in a family that taught you that being good meant making others happy, these questions will arise whenever you must decide between doing what you want or what others expect of you. Even if you weren't taught this definition of goodness, these questions are likely to perplex you. Our society sends confusing and contradictory messages about responsibilities to ourselves and others.

We're taught to tell the truth. But we're also taught that we shouldn't be honest if it will hurt someone's feelings.

We're taught to love our neighbors. But we're also taught to be wary of strangers.

We're taught that selfishness and greed are wrong. Yet almost everyone yearns to be rich.

We're taught to value kindness and compassion. But we're also taught first and foremost to take care of our own.

No wonder we sometimes find it hard to decide when to act as our "brother's keeper" and when to "look out for number one." Following are some tools that will help you determine when it's right for you to change—even if it affects others.

Protection vs. Manipulation

Have you ever refrained from making a change because you had to protect another person? In hindsight, is it possible that you were really protecting yourself from feeling guilty? That's often the case. There are, however, better ways to cope with guilt.

Ask yourself what you would want if the situation were reversed. Would you want someone you love to turn down an opportunity because he or she thought you needed protection? How would you expect him or her to feel about you after making a sacrifice on your behalf? How would you feel about their deciding what *you* needed without consulting you?

If you've ever found out that someone lied to you in order to "protect" you, you probably felt angry, patronized, and betrayed. You'd rather have known the truth and dealt with it, no matter how difficult, than lived with an illusion. We resent being lied to because we know other people aren't protecting us. They're protecting themselves from having to deal with our *response* to the truth. That's not protection. That's manipulation.

It's easy to see the manipulation when someone else is protecting us from the truth. It's harder to see it in our own behavior. After all, no one wants to hurt people they love. But you're bound to some of the time. Whether you're changing careers, leaving home, or asserting your honest opinions for the first time, these actions will affect everyone close to you, to good or ill effect.

There's a difference, however, between trying to hurt people and taking actions on your own behalf that others find hurtful. The former you can control, the latter you can't. No matter what you do—or don't do—you will never be able to control other people's feelings in response to your behavior. You can, however, listen to their feelings and accept them. You don't have to like their feelings, prove them "wrong," or admit you were "bad" to trigger them. If you can accept their feelings while holding firm to your course of action, the change that you initiated becomes a prod toward greater honesty, individuality, and independence for everyone in the family.

When Loved Ones Overreact to Your Change

Are you afraid that changes you make will have consequences more serious than hurting someone's feelings? That someone you love may become depressed? Return to drugs or drinking? Have a nervous breakdown or a heart attack? Is preserving the status quo staving off disaster for someone else? If these are your fears, ask yourself:

> Are you equipped to serve as your loved one's psychotherapist, physician, spiritual advisor, psychopharmacologist, or addiction counselor?

It's impossible to fill these roles effectively with people you love. You're too close. You can't see their strengths or their problems objectively. Instead of helping them, you risk shoring up strategies of procrastination and denial, and fostering dependence rather than responsibility.

Serious Problems Require Professional Help

If loved ones are depressed, they need a therapist or an antidepressant. If they're in danger of a heart attack, they need a cardiologist. If they're addicted to drugs or alcohol, they need a treatment program or a twelve-step sponsor. These problems are serious. They merit your concern and empathy. But they aren't caused by and can't be cured by changes you make—or don't make.

Watching loved ones experience pain is hellish. But the most caring action you can take is to point them in the direction of the skilled help they require. Then steel yourself to wait and hope for the best. And in the meantime, focus your energy on the one responsibility you and you alone can and must fulfill—which is to manage your own life as best as you can.

"I SHOULD FORCE MYSELF TO CHANGE"

Is willpower the key to achieving your goals? You may think so if you grew up in a family in which discipline was valued at the expense of spontaneity, impulsiveness, and intuition. You may have learned to equate

- Flexibility with laxity
- Creativity with disorder
- Playfulness with mental and moral decline

Willpower serves as the reliable, efficient dictator of the unruly troops of emotion, imagination, and dreams. When your will commands, these psychic soldiers should stand alert and obey. If they don't, you must be lazy, weak, and undisciplined.

When you're stalled or frustrated in achieving your goals, you'll assume discipline is what you need. Like an impatient boss, you'll try to whip yourself into shape. You'll make rules, set schedules, establish routines, blow whistles, and devise punishments for disorderly conduct. Yet ironically, the harder you try to bully yourself into submission, the more defiant and disorganized your behavior is likely to become. The danger is that you'll become disheartened, declare yourself weak and lazy, and give up. The problem, however, isn't the weakness of your will. It's that you have given your will powers it isn't designed to exercise.

Willpower Is Your Ally, Not Your Boss

Discipline is an important asset in achieving goals. But it's only helpful when you're working toward a goal you're sure you want. Willpower has to serve goals; it can't set them. Frankly, as much respect as your inner tyrant may have received when you were growing up, its dirty little secret is that it isn't very bright—it can't get the job done without help from the unruly troops. It doesn't know enough about you. If you're hesitating on the brink of change, feel unmotivated, sabotage schedules, and break your rules, these are clues to inner conflict. You need to pay attention to them, not subdue them. If you try, you'll discover what all bullies eventually do—tyranny lasts only so long before rebellion strikes.

You Can't Win a Fight with Yourself, So Declare a Cease-Fire

You can't win a fight with yourself. You can only tire, confuse, and demoralize yourself. You have to declare a cease-fire, and resolve to adopt a more democratic and egalitarian policy toward the different parts of you—even the unruly, unpredictable, impractical, emotional, and impulsive ones. They are as much a part of you as the analytical, practical, serious, and organized ones. You have to consult them all before you set your goals.

The inner voices you devalue or disapprove of won't be silenced by willpower. They will clamor for attention. You have to listen and learn, and assume they have something valuable to tell you about whether or not the goals you're trying to force upon yourself are your heart's desires. Only then will you be able to determine what your inner majority really wants. At that point, willpower can serve as your ally, not your boss.

"IF I CAN'T BE THE BEST, I SHOULDN'T TRY"

Did your family encourage you to "play to win" with siblings, cousins, and classmates? If so, you may have learned that proving you were better than others was the most important goal. Your ego may be satisfied with nothing less than first place. If you can't win, why bother trying? Anything less is humiliating. Second place is tantamount to failure. Society conspires to reinforce a "winner take all" mentality. After all, who remembers Olympians who bring home silver or bronze medals rather than gold?

Winning may become more important than whether you *like* what you're doing. The danger of having to be the best is that it can lock you into only doing things that you can be best at. You won't be able to try new things. You won't be able to take pleasure in anything you just do "well." Being "average" at anything would be unthinkable. This barrier is especially distressing at midlife, when the quest to fulfill delayed dreams causes many people to yearn for dramatic renewal in their careers. No matter how stifled you may feel in your current profession—and no matter how strong the tug to begin a new career—you'll balk at the prospect of starting over if you think it will prove you're a loser.

New Priorities

There are more important priorities than being the best:

- Finding the *courage* to try new things.
- Developing the *patience* to learn from mistakes.
- Mining the *self-knowledge* derived from following your curiosity.
- Building the *strength* to hang on to these priorities even when it seems as though everyone else is still playing to win.

If you commit to these priorities, you will always be the best at the only game that counts—finding out who you truly are, and molding your life to fit.

"IT'S TOO LATE FOR ME TO CHANGE"

Did you watch older generations in your family settle into predictable routines and diminished expectations in the second half of life? The belief that getting older means you shouldn't begin anything new is the saddest barrier to change. It rests upon the assumption that new opportunities belong to youth, and that aging means resigning yourself to the familiar, the predictable, the lost chance.

The underlying assumption is that you shouldn't waste energy and resources on starting a new career unless you'll have time to produce a certain volume of work. According to this utilitarian view, education and work derive their primary value from the amount you contribute to others. In other words, the pleasure or growth you derive from working and learning is secondary—they are means, not ends in themselves.

It's Never Too Late to Learn New Things

What matters at any age isn't how much you produce, it's how you live your life. It's never too late to learn new things or develop new skills. The worth of an endeavor is proportionate not to how much time you spend on it or how much it contributes to others, but on the amount of joy and absorption you experience in the midst of it. That joy and absorption is in itself a contribution to others, because when you love your life, you embody love and you inspire all whose lives you touch to strive for what you've attained.

A vibrant, creative "older" person—keeping in mind that, depending on your audience, that age can range from forty to eighty—becomes an especially important role model in a society such as ours, which is both phobic about age and aging rapidly as baby boomers hit fifty and beyond. Every single older person who affirms his or her right to strive for happiness throughout life liberates us all from the mindless, cruel, and wasteful stranglehold of ageism. To devalue age is to devalue life itself. After all, from the moment we are born, what else do we *do* besides get older?

13

Exorcising Family Ghosts That Haunt the Workplace

Have you ever encountered a colleague, client, or boss whose behavior enraged you, rendered you speechless, or wounded you with surprising power and depth? Their behavior wasn't abusive, illegal, or unethical, but you found it irritating, insulting, or disorienting in the extreme. In response, did you feel confused about what to do? Did you feel preoccupied with the interaction, unable to let it go, and unable to follow others' good advice—much less locate your own? If so, you may have exported an early familial role into the workplace, and you've gotten stuck in familiar patterns. You may feel at such times as though family ghosts are haunting you at work in the guise of your boss, employees, or peers.

The telltale signs that conflicts at work stem from replaying family roles include:

- **Intense emotions,** disproportionate to the triggering behavior.
- **Wide-ranging emotions,** from vulnerability to fury.
- **Confusion or helplessness**—you either cannot think of a plan of action or cannot bring yourself to execute it.
- **"Something" about** the colleague or boss that's hard to define but gets under your skin prevents you from setting limits, staying focused, or brushing off comments or behavior as you would if it were someone else.

These situations differ from those in which bosses or colleagues are clearly behaving abusively. As discussed in **chapter 10,** survivors of abuse may struggle to see and protect themselves from abuse, but abuse is always the responsibility of the abuser. In these less extreme, everyday conflicts at work, the challenge is not to determine who is responsible, it's to find new and effective strategies for resolving the problem.

WHY REPLAYING FAMILY ROLES CONTRIBUTES TO WORKPLACE CONFLICTS

Playing a role means following a set of unwritten rules that define appropriate—and inappropriate—behavior. If you played the role of caretaker, for example, you were expected to respond empathically to the needs of others. You weren't expected to rebel, to act selfishly, or to give commands. You'll excel in the skills of listening and extending support to others. But you probably won't have experience in protecting yourself from being taken advantage of, in directing and evaluating other people, or in forcefully asserting your opinions. Yet in the workplace, you need these latter skills.

The roles you played for your family—and the relationship skills that accompanied them—shape the quality of your experience in the workplace. You'll thrive when work draws upon skills you've practiced and perfected growing up. You'll feel frustration, pain, and confusion when work requires skills that you never learned, never practiced, and that break the rules of your family roles.

Workplaces Are Not Families

Families are organizations with hierarchies. As in a business or nonprofit organization, members must recognize authority, follow commands, and collaborate on shared goals. Our first models for the roles of leader, follower, and teammate are other family members. It's natural for us to export our family's "rules" about authority, teamwork, and leadership into the workplace. But workplaces are not families. You can't count on being loved, accepted, or indulged by bosses and colleagues. Nor are you bonded by biological or adoptive ties to your workplace. On the other hand, families are not governed by written policies and laws of fairness, rights, and respect, and workplaces are—or should be.

Workplace conflicts commonly arise from one of two situations:

- When you expect others in the workplace to accept or share your family's rules about leadership and teamwork, but they don't, leaving you unsure how to behave.
- When you respond to workplace conflicts in familiar ways—such as clamming up, running away, or rebelling—instead of looking for constructive ways to communicate about and resolve the problem.

You can benefit from identifying the source of workplace conflicts in family roles in the following ways.

- Tracing the conflict to the past reduces the sting of current rejection, insult, or injury.
- Expanding your repertoire of relationship skills beyond those practiced and refined in your family equips you to solve a wider range of problems.
- Clarifying that the problem isn't "in" you or in the other person—but stems from a breakdown in communication in the relationship—boosts morale and confidence.

SOLVING COMMON PROBLEMS IN AUTHORITY, TEAMWORK, AND LEADERSHIP

Descriptions follow of common problems in authority, teamwork, and leadership. See if you recognize conflicts you've encountered. If so, identify which family rules must be altered, and which relationship skills you need to solve each problem.

AUTHORITY

Difficulty Speaking Out to Your Boss: When Parental Authority Was Used to Berate

When Jill was ten years old and "clammed up and stalked off" from her mother's overbearing criticism, her behavior fit well with the role she played in her family—that of a stubborn, recalcitrant child. The rules in her family dictated that parents had the authority to berate children under the guise of "correcting" their behavior. Children were not allowed to "talk back" or "correct" authority. Jill's stony withdrawals were her only allowable protection from her mother's verbal onslaughts. But in the workplace, Jill's coping strategy communicates a stubborn reluctance to learn. Although untrue, this impression will hurt Jill's career if she can't correct it.

Now a customer service manager, Jill felt aggravated and hurt by her boss's gruff style of feedback. Her boss always began evaluations with detailed negative comments and skimmed over positive comments at the end—by then, Jill was too upset to hear them. Jill's friends advised her to suggest that her boss begin evaluations with details about Jill's successes. But Jill felt reduced to silent, smoldering rage when her boss began to speak. She found herself "clamming up and stalking off" instead of solving the problem.

Find Your Voice

If you weren't allowed to talk back to authority, you'll need to find your voice, not to talk back to your boss, but to *educate* him or her about what you need to work effectively. You'll also need to develop three important skills:

First, *distinguish* between the constraints on your behavior as a child and the freedom you have as an adult to assert yourself.

Second, *speak out* on your own behalf when authority is being used in ways that block your learning instead of helping you grow.

Third, *communicate* clearly to authority how you learn best—what amount and style of performance feedback enables you to do your best work.

Defying Authority: When Parental Authority Was Used to Shame

Dale's father would review in detail every single mistake his son made, whether it was in his math homework, mowing the grass, or washing the car. His corrections went on long after Dale had identified his error. Dale felt humiliated by his father's minute focus on flaws. His only protection was to strive for perfection and avoid giving his father the opportunity to shame him for mistakes.

Dale learned that authorities were sadistic enforcers of the goal of perfection. Because he saw mistakes as symptoms of inadequacy, he was unable to recognize or benefit from feedback aimed at helping him to learn. His resentment of authority was exacerbated by the rules his family taught about apology—that it demonstrated submission to others and was the equivalent of crying "Uncle." For Dale, therefore, apologizing meant further humiliation.

As a public relations writer, Dale responded belligerently to his boss's editorial suggestions, and ignored her warnings about insubordination. His boss frequently told Dale he was a promising writer. But Dale felt humiliated by even minor corrections to his work, since they implied it was imperfect. Instead of accepting authority, he defied his boss and sent a fund-raising letter directly to donors. Even though Dale's letter alienated donors, he refused to apologize to his boss. At that point, Dale was fired.

Learn from Legitimate Authority—And from Your Mistakes

If you learned to view authority—even legitimate authority intended to guide and teach you—as an exertion of power over you, designed to humiliate you for flaws in your performance, you'll benefit from these important skills:

First, *acknowledge* that some authority is trustworthy and benign, and that constructive feedback can help you learn—not embarrass you.

Second, *view mistakes as opportunities* for growth, and view continuous learning—not perfection—as the goal of work.

Third, *redefine apology* as a sign of strength, flexibility, and consideration for others, not weakness.

Needing to Be Special to Your Boss: When Parental Authority Was Tied to Approval and Affection

Becky's parents used their authority to manipulate her into obeying and pleasing them. When she complied with their wishes, they would lavish her with praise and favors. When she followed her own wishes, they barely acknowledged her presence. Instead of learning to derive pride and self-esteem from independent achievements, Becky derived them from achieving her parents' approval. She continued this pattern in the workplace—seeking "special" status and approval from authorities, based not on the quality of her work but on her willingness to please. The cost of being special was high, however. She had to give up her own goals, and the esteem and trust of peers.

When Becky became an assistant professor at a university, she found older mentors to help advance her career. She received many benefits from a senior professor who helped her find research funding and teaching assignments. His approval, however, was contingent upon Becky following his advice. When she pursued her own ideas, he threatened to withdraw his support. Being special was important to Becky's self-esteem, but it limited her independence. It also made her the object of colleagues' resentment. They believed her advancement was based on "sucking up," not on merit.

Distinguish Between Approval and Authority

If you need personal approval, attention, "special" or favored status from your boss, you need to unhook approval from authority. You will thereby liberate your self-esteem from being held hostage by people who want to manipulate you. Adopt these skills:

First, *distinguish* between personal approval and professional evaluations of your work.

Second, *seek* mentors who respect your autonomy and support *your* goals. Avoid anyone who expects you to substitute his or her goals for your own.

Third, *shift the basis of self-esteem* to your own assessment of your work, knowledge, ethics, and character—and divorce it from seeking anyone else's approval.

TEAMWORK

Avoiding Teamwork: When Treating Everyone the Same Means Ignoring Individuality

Monica's parents were so determined to treat her and her two sisters equally that they bought them the same clothes and gave them the same allowance. Rather than give them individual gifts of equal value, her parents gave them exactly the same gifts. In short, everyone got what no one wanted. The result wasn't sibling harmony, but exacerbated rivalry. Each sibling felt fiercely protective of her individuality, and ferociously competitive with her sisters for recognition of their differences. Being a team player to Monica meant forsaking her uniqueness and being treated by management as just like everyone else.

Now a research scientist, Monica hates teamwork. She despises having her work blurred with others', fearing that she'll be blamed for their faults and lose credit for her own ideas. She chose research as a career so she could work as an individual contributor. Following national trends in management, however, executives in her firm now require cross-functional teamwork from everyone—even mavericks in the R&D department. She can't avoid teams anymore, but Monica feels anxious and impatient at the prospect of "mushing" her work with that of others.

Combining Individuality with Teamwork

If you fear losing your identity in a group, you may have to alter your assumptions about teamwork. Collaboration doesn't have to equal loss of identity. To the contrary, teams work best when members' contributions complement but do not duplicate one another. These skills will help you approach teamwork with greater confidence.

First, *view teams as collaborations of individuals* making distinct contributions to a shared goal. Your goal is shared—not necessarily your ideas, your expertise, or opinions.

Second, *clarify* how teamwork can benefit you as an individual—by lightening your workload, giving you access to others' perspectives, and increasing your effectiveness.

Third, *expand your pride* in individual achievements to include the unique contribution you make to a group.

Taking On Too Much: When Your Team Is Only You

Bart grew up with three brothers, all of whom would squabble over chores. Eventually, his mother would tire of their bickering and declare, "All right, if none of you are willing to help me, I'll do it myself!" Bart was the only sibling who felt guilty enough at the sight of his mother mowing the grass, washing the dishes, or weeding the garden to take over from her. His brothers would go on playing, and his mother would thank Bart for being her one "good boy."

Bart disliked both his brothers' laziness and his mother's martyrly tone. He felt stuck doing more than his fair share of chores, but he had no authority over his brothers. He hoped desperately for one of two things: either his brothers would develop compassion and responsibility or his mother would develop backbone and order her sons to obey her. Neither ever happened.

Now a manager for a courier service, Bart works on several teams. In each, he's the first to "break down" and volunteer to chair meetings, keep minutes, or write reports. He feels overburdened and resentful of his teammates' willingness to let him do more than his fair share. He volunteers because he doesn't want to let down the upper management of his firm, but he himself feels let down by their failure to step in and "save" him from his colleagues' laziness. He feels besieged, betrayed, and angry. Once again, he feels stuck, without the authority to change either his peers or upper management.

Do Your Fair Share—Not Others'

If you typically take on more than your fair share because colleagues and supervisors depend upon you to be the "good" worker, then you need to change the rules of teamwork:

First, *distinguish* between doing a fair amount of good work and being judged as good because you do more than your fair share. Insist upon the former, and refuse the latter—it's exploitation.

Second, *overcome the temptation to "save"* colleagues and supervisors from the problem of unbalanced workloads and unmotivated teams. Overburdening yourself won't solve the problem, but it may prevent others from noticing or taking action.

Third, *complain* about unfairness—clearly, politely, but firmly. And continue complaining until someone listens and takes action.

LEADERSHIP

Difficulty Asserting Authority: When Leadership Was Intrusive

Terry's parents micromanaged their children. They didn't just assign Terry a task and let her do it at her own pace and style. She had to perform it at a certain time, in a particular order, with very precise outcomes. She was acutely conscious of carrying out her parents' precise instructions when performing chores, so much so that she never felt any ownership, creativity, or pride in doing them. Their commands felt oppressive, dictatorial, and intrusive. She resented their orders and feared behaving like them so much she pointedly avoided applying for supervisory roles.

Eventually, to get the salary she wanted, Terry could no longer avoid accepting promotion to a supervisory position with the community agency where she worked. In this position, she felt self-conscious and inhibited about telling other people—especially those older than she—what to do. She feared being perceived as bossy, power hungry, and insensitive. Her greatest fear was that she would find out she actually liked "throwing her weight around" and become a tyrant.

Leaders Serve Those Who Choose to Follow

If you fear exerting power over people you supervise, you need to redefine your task as leader. Follow these steps:

First, *distinguish between dictatorship and leadership.* Dictators coerce; they gain effectiveness through raw power. Leaders gain effectiveness by understanding what people need in order to do good work.

Second, *ask what they need.* Your task is to empower the people you want to lead to do good work by providing what they need. If you're not sure you're giving it, ask again.

Third, *identify leaders* who have inspired you, and use them as models while you experiment with your own style of leadership. Determine the balance of flexibility and firmness that seems fair and respectful to you.

Fourth, *adopt a "no fault" stance toward leadership.* As hard as you try, you'll never please everyone. Those who *choose* to do so will follow you, others will choose to leave. It doesn't necessarily mean that you or they have done anything wrong.

Inability to Delegate: When Leadership Was Demanded Too Soon

Marshall grew up with two younger brothers. His parents expected him to supervise his siblings. Marshall was held accountable for the quality of their homework, for their being dressed for school on time, and for their overall "good" behavior. If his brothers refused to do their chores, Marshall was punished. Marshall, however, had no effective means of disciplining his siblings. He was given responsibility for his brothers' behavior before he was old enough to have authority over them. Responsibility without commensurate authority guarantees stress—and that's exactly Marshall's response as an adult to the challenge of leadership.

When Marshall was hired as a graphic designer for an ad agency, he lobbied his budget director for an assistant for two years. Yet now that he has one, he can't delegate. Giving his assistant tasks feels like "giving body parts away." What if she doesn't do the work correctly, he wonders. Will others judge his work based on her output? What if he has to waste precious time correcting her work? Where will he find the time to figure out what to tell her to do in the first place? Ironically, Marshall feels more stressed by having an assistant than he did without one.

Clarify What Your Responsibilities Are—And Aren't

If delegating tasks makes you anxious and fearful that you will lose control and be judged and punished for others' work, you need to clarify your responsibilities as a leader:

First, *make sure that the reach of your authority fits the grasp of your responsibilities.* In other words, clarify that you have credible authority over the people you supervise.

Second, *take responsibility* for delegating tasks fairly and clearly. Establish a time frame and criteria for evaluation.

Third, *give responsibility* to others to get the job done on time and according to standards you've agreed upon, but then back off and trust them do the work.

Fourth, *give praise and/or corrective feedback* as needed. Refrain from doing work over again "your way." Respect others' goals and styles of learning, and make sure your feedback reflects this.

YOU CAN EXORCISE YOUR GHOSTS

The challenge of exorcising ghosts from your workplace is that they show up so quickly and frequently. All it takes to evoke old family patterns is a co-worker whose mannerisms, speech, or behavior mimic those of a parent, older sibling, or others from the past. Once triggered, emotions stemming from hurts and insults long past—but never healed—obscure your vision of present choices.

In order to restore clear vision of the present, you have to discern and purge these mischievous ghosts. The good news is that family ghosts disappear in the "light" of your awareness. Once you understand the source and intensity of your feelings, their power dims. You can focus once again on the ways your workplace and your colleagues are different from your family members and your past. This shift of focus enables you to see the range of choices available to you as an adult, and enables you to regain your ability to communicate, collaborate, and strategize solutions to your problems.

Part Four

Living Your Own Dream: 7 Steps to Reclaim Your Career

✦

14

Step 1: Define Your Purpose in Exploring Family Influences

The seven steps in this part of the book will help you understand the following:

- How your family history has influenced your career in positive and/or negative ways
- What you as an individual need and want from work
- The values and beliefs that will help you attain what you want
- How to establish a flexible but structured plan to achieve your goals

The exercises in each step were designed to be done in sequence, from the first through the last. Each chapter includes a section headed "About the Exercise," which provides specific instructions for answering the questions that follow.

These exercises ask you to reflect upon and write about your family's past and your own, and to envision your future. You'll probably want to record your observations in a notebook, and to regularly read back through your answers and add additional insights or questions that occur to you.

Think of working on these exercises as digging down through the layers of an archeological site composed of your own and your family's work history. At first, you may not recognize what the different artifacts/memories you encounter have to do with one another. But as you continue digging and more layers and artifacts come into view, and you allow your intuition to range freely over the site, gradually the relationship of the parts to the whole will become clear. Be patient. Dig slowly. Over time, the fragments of your family's history will reveal their connections to one another—and to your own reasons for digging.

DEFINE YOUR PURPOSE

To gain the most from exploring your family history, you need to clarify:

- **What** answers you're seeking
- **Why** you're motivated to look for them now
- **How** you want to apply this knowledge

In this chapter, Exercise 14-1, "Define Your Purpose," will help you to answer these questions.

DON'T BE SURPRISED IF YOU HESITATE INITIALLY

Even if you're ready with your head to explore your family's influence on your career, don't be surprised if your gut hesitates at the brink. If you're like most people, you'll wonder whether you'll regret unearthing difficult facts and challenging feelings. Almost everyone begins this journey with two contrasting impulses: a compelling hunch that the answers they need to build satisfying work lives lie within their family history and reluctance to follow the hunch to its source.

Your hesitation is natural. It springs from awareness that this exploration is likely to cause change. Remember, you *want* change. If you spell out below why you picked up this book, you can reassure yourself of the benefits you're seeking. Everyone I've known who explored family influences on their career development has been glad in the long run for the clarity, freedom, confidence, and independence they gained from their search.

DETERMINE "WHY NOW?"

The desire to understand family history is often triggered by an experience that forces you to admit something is false or out of balance in your life. The trigger signals a need for answers that go beyond changing jobs or studying labor trends—or anything you can learn from external sources. The following exercise asks you to determine what is nudging you to undertake this exploration now. It's like having an itch—you have to find the source in order to know where to scratch.

Do These Triggers Apply to You?

For many, the passage into midlife provides a trigger. The hard truth settles in that if you don't get around to making your dreams come true, no one else will do it for you. Other triggers include:

- Losses of all kinds—death, illness, divorce, injury, separation
- Being laid off, "downsized," demoted, or otherwise forced to seek new career options—and to reexamine values and goals
- The positive effects of psychotherapy, meditation, or other types of spiritual renewal, which stimulate a craving for greater meaning in life
- The good fortune of finding friends, partners, or teachers who affirm your right to happiness and nurture the courage to change

Whether it's something you lost, something you found, or something that shifted while you weren't paying attention, something inside you has changed. What is it?

WHERE AND HOW HAVE YOU LOOKED BEFORE NOW?

Answering this question will help you understand how you try to solve problems, and how you might benefit from trying new strategies. To whom (partner, friend, pastor, counselor, etc.) or to what (books, tests, courses, etc.) have you instinctively turned? Clarifying what you haven't yet learned from usual resources will clarify the benefits of trying "unusual" ones—such as exploring your family's past!

ABOUT THE EXERCISE

This exercise invites you to identify the questions you want to answer about your career, your family history, or your life in general. Keep these on hand as you complete Steps 2 to 7 in the chapters that follow, and use them like the outline of a jigsaw puzzle to frame the pieces of information you gather. At the end of each of the remaining steps, you will find an exercise, "Before You Take the Next Step," that asks you to review the picture taking shape within your "frame."

✦ ✦ ✦ ✦ ✦

EXERCISE 14-1 *Define Your Purpose*

WHY NOW?

Why did you pick up this book *now*?
What recent inner or outer events have affected your feelings about your job, your career, or your family?
What questions are you trying to answer? (Try responding to this question three times. Each time ask yourself, "What *deeper* questions am I asking?")

WHERE AND HOW HAVE YOU LOOKED—AND NOT LOOKED?

Where or how else have you looked? (people, books, classes, self-assessment tests, job-hunting workshops, networking opportunities, etc.)
Why did you choose these resources?
What did you learn from these resources?
What have you not yet learned that you hope to find here?
What resources have you avoided or underutilized? Why?

HOW WILL FINDING THE ANSWERS CHANGE YOU?

How will finding the answers to your questions change you?
What are your worst fears about these changes?
How realistic are your fears?
If they became real, how would you deal with them?
How will these changes benefit you?

15

Step 2: Explore Your Family's Work History

Exploring your family's work history clarifies the influences that have shaped your career. Step 2 includes two exercises. The first, "Family Work History," asks you to gather information about your parents' and grandparents' educational and professional achievements, ambitions, frustrations, and disappointments, and to reflect upon the impact these events have had on your life.

The second exercise, "Dialogue with a Dead or Absent Relative," clarifies the influence of relatives you're unable to speak to or learn about directly. In this exercise you evoke the person's presence and tap your intuitive knowledge of his or her emotional significance. You can use this exercise to illuminate the inner presence—both the inner being and the presence inside you—of any relative.

ABOUT THE EXERCISES

These exercises cover a lot of family history. Don't try to answer all the questions at once. Do them bit by bit, and reread your answers in-between sittings, adding new observations or insights that occur to you. Take plenty of time, and don't worry about getting the "right" answers. When it comes to family stories, there usually are few facts and many versions, depending on who's talking. Never mind—listen to them all. Give yourself time to digest different points of view, and unifying themes will appear. Trust your instincts to ferret out the emotional truth that makes sense of the facts as you know them. Reviewing **chapters 6, 7,** and **8** will help you think through your answers.

The exercises inquire about parents and grandparents. Remember, these categories aren't restricted to biological or adoptive ties, but refer to the people who were primarily responsible for raising and taking care of you, and teaching you right from wrong. Include in the exercise the people who were emotionally connected to you in this way, whether they are technically relatives or not.

FOLLOW YOUR CURIOSITY

Although all the questions are useful, they may not all feel useful to you right now. Begin with the questions you're drawn to. You can return to the others later. If you try to force your way through all the questions in order, you may become tired, frustrated, or bored. These reactions will block you from learning. Be easy, gentle, and lighthearted as you go. Take frequent breaks. Follow your curiosity, and you'll find the answers you need.

CONSULT EXTENDED FAMILY

If you run into gaps in your knowledge of your family's history, consult your parents and extended family members to obtain the missing information. If your parents are reluctant to answer or say they don't know, try consulting a more distant relative, one you may not be as close to and wouldn't ordinarily seek out. They may have information your parents don't have access to. Or, after they find out you're talking to other relatives, your parents may be motivated to provide more details and "set the record straight."

TRUST YOUR INTUITION

If you don't know the answer, write down your hunches. Your emotional history within your family has given you intimate knowledge of your family's dreams, desires, losses, and hopes whether you have ever articulated them or not, and whether other family members verify them or not. Facts and events from your family's history are less important than the emotional impact they left behind on individual members. You have been surrounded by this impact every day of your life. Trust your intuition.

✦ ✦ ✦ ✦ ✦

EXERCISE 15-1 *Family Work History*

GRANDPARENTS

Educational and Career Goals

What were each of your grandparents' educational and career goals?

Were these their own goals, or goals handed to them by others within the family?

Which goals did they achieve? Who or what helped them to do so?

Which goals were they unable to achieve?

Why not? (family barriers, poverty, illness, emotional problems, sexism, racism, the Depression, military service, historical events, etc.)

Self-Esteem, Values, and Beliefs

What effect did these successes and failures have on how your grandparents felt about themselves? (proud, embarrassed, frustrated, defeated, etc.)

What effect did these successes and failures have on how the rest of the family viewed them? (legendary heroes, miserable failures, reliable backbone, etc.)

What effect did these successes and failures have on their values and beliefs about the purpose of work, the meaning of success, and the significance of money?

Which of these values and beliefs did they pass on to your parents?

Expectations of Your Parents

What did your grandparents expect of your mother/father (answer for each separately) when they were growing up? (intelligence, achievement, skill level, industriousness, obedience, etc.)

What "job assignments" did your grandparents assign your parents, both inside and outside the family? (mediator, troublemaker, hero, "junior" parent to younger siblings, inherit the family business, never leave home, etc.)

How did your mother/father respond to their parents' expectations? (compliance, rebellion, running away, etc.)

PARENTS

Childhood Dreams

When your parents were growing up, what did each dream of becoming?

What appealed to them about these dreams?

How were these dreams viewed by their families? (ridiculed, supported, encouraged, ignored, etc.)

Did they achieve these dreams? Why or why not?

Gender and Sibling Position

How were your mother's/father's family "job assignments" influenced by gender?

How were they influenced by sibling position?

Were there family roles or "job assignments" your parent wanted but was disqualified from because of gender or sibling position?

How did your parent respond to being disqualified from the "job" he or she wanted? (envy or rivalry with siblings; blame and anger at one or both parents; self-doubt; etc.)

What would your mother/father say they wished had been different about what their parents expected of them? Why?

What difference would it have made in their educational and career goals? Why?

What difference would it have made in what they expected from you? Why?

Education

How well did your mother/father do in school?

Did they get more, less, or different schooling than they wanted? Why?

If your mother/father were able to return to school today to study whatever they wished, what would they choose? Why?

Career Goals

When they were young adults, what were your mother's and father's career aspirations?

Were these their own goals, or goals handed to them by others within the family?

Which goals did they achieve? Who or what helped them to do so?

Which goals were they unable to achieve?

Why not?

Did their goals change over the course of their adult lives? How? Why?

Successes and Regrets

What achievements would your mother/father say they are proudest of in their lives? (good parent, financially secure, writing a novel, taking care of others, etc.)

How are these achievements similar to and different from what they set out to achieve when they were younger?

If different, what changed for your parents?

What dreams, goals, or plans would your mother/father say they had failed to fulfill, or felt disappointed in the outcome? (Not necessarily what they would say aloud, but what you know to be true in their hearts.)

If your mother/father were given a second chance at living their lives, what would they chose to do this time?

YOU

Direct Requests—What You Were Encouraged to Do

When you were growing up, what school subjects, extracurricular activities, and/or future college or career goals did your parents directly encourage you to pursue? (i.e., they openly, verbally told you to do it)

How did you respond to your parents' encouragement? (trusted their judgment completely, complied out of fear, became oppositional, etc.)

At the time, how did they describe the reasons they encouraged you in these directions? (they didn't need a reason; it's your family "duty," your "genes," or your "destiny," etc.)

What did you think of those reasons at the time?

In hindsight, what do you think motivated your parents to encourage you in these directions?

How did you benefit from being encouraged in these directions? (at the time or later in life)

In what ways was encouragement in these directions difficult for you? (at the time or later in life)

What alternative directions, if any, do you wish your parents had directly encouraged you to pursue?

What difference would these alternatives have made for you then? Now?

Direct Requests—What You Were Discouraged from Doing

What subjects, activities, or future education/career goals did your parents directly discourage you from pursuing?

How did they discourage you and what did they say to justify it? (ridiculed it, declared it dangerous or improper, threatened to withdraw financial support for a "waste of time," etc.)

How did you respond?

What did you think of their reasons at the time?

In hindsight, what do you think motivated their discouragement?

What subjects or skills were or still are dormant or underdeveloped in you as a result of this discouragement?

Indirect Requests

When you were growing up, how much freedom did your parents' *say* you had to choose your own activities and goals? (e.g., "Do whatever will make you happy . . .")

How much freedom did you actually feel you had?

In what areas (academics, sports, career plans) did you feel less free to choose for yourself?

Looking backward, what indirect signals were you "reading" in your parents' behavior or tone? (lack of enthusiasm, sighs, withdrawal of affection, etc.)

At the time, how did you interpret these "mixed messages"?

How do you interpret them today?

How did these indirect signals influence your "choices" in these areas?

Your Name

Were you named after a family member? What expectations did you inherit with your name?

Are you seen by family members as having lived up (or "lived down") to your namesake? Why or why not?

What have been the benefits and drawbacks of these expectations?

Were you named after someone else (real or fictional)? Why?

What expectations came with your name?

What have been the benefits and drawbacks of these expectations?

If you weren't named after someone, why did your parents select your name?

What qualities or personal characteristics did it represent to them?

What have been the benefits and drawbacks of having this name?

Your Gender and Sibling Order

What were your family roles or "job assignments" inside and outside the family? (over- or underachiever, mediator, scapegoat, etc.)
Why were *you* chosen for these "jobs"?
What did you like or dislike about your family "job"?
What skills and responsibilities did these assignments require you to develop?
How do these skills and responsibilities show up in your career path?
What effect did your gender and sibling position have on qualifying you for these assignments?
Were there assignments you were disqualified for because of your gender or sibling position?
Were any of these assignments ones you would have preferred to your own? Why?
At the time, how did you feel about being disqualified?
How did you feel at the time about the sibling(s) who had the job(s) you would have preferred?
How do you currently feel about these siblings?
What skills and responsibilities would these other jobs have required you to develop?
How did your family's view of your "qualifications" and "disqualifications" influence your perspective on which careers were possible or impossible for you?
How do your family's views currently influence your perspective on which careers are possible or impossible for you?

Triangles: If You Had to "Choose Sides"

Did your parents disagree about your academic and career goals?
What did they disagree about? Why?
What form did their disagreements take? (shouting matches, debates, not talking to each other, sabotage, bribery, etc.)
How were you affected by their disagreements? (tried to mediate, find compromises, fought with them both, etc.)
Did you have to choose between them? How did you pick?
What effect did it have on you to have to choose (then and now)?
What effect did being chosen have on your relationship with the "chosen" parent (then and now)?
What effect did not being "chosen" have on your other parent (then and now)?

How did other family members interpret your "choice" (then and now)?

How did it affect your relationships with siblings—then and now?

What effect did the forced choice have on your career options?

In retrospect, what do you believe motivated your parents to fight over and through you?

What difference would it have made for you in the past if you could have been equally close to both parents?

What difference would it make for you now?

What would you have to give up for this to happen—and what would you gain?

What would other family members have to give up—and what would they gain?

Triangles: If Your Parents Did the Choosing

Was one of your parents closer to you or more involved with your educational and career goals than the other?

How was this closeness explained within the family? (same gender, "natural" similarities, etc.)

How was your distance from the other parent explained?

At the time, how did you understand both the closeness and the distance?

What have been the benefits and drawbacks of the closeness and the distance (then and now)?

How did the closeness and distance affect your relationships with your siblings (then and now)?

What effect did the closeness/distance have on your career options?

In retrospect, what unresolved conflict between your parents was being solved by involving you in a triangle?

What difference would it have made for you in the past if you could have been equally close to both parents?

What would have been different in their relationship?

What would have been different in your relationships with siblings?

What difference would it make for you if you could be equally close today?

What would you have to give up for this to happen—and what would you gain?

What would other family members have to give up—and what would they gain?

✦ ✦ ✦ ✦ ✦

Exercise 15-2 *Dialogue with a Dead or Absent Relative*

First, identify the person you want to communicate with. You may have an obvious choice. If not, ask yourself what family members you feel drawn to "talk" to. Accept whoever comes to mind, even if you don't know what you want to discuss. You may not be able to understand before you do the exercise what significance the person has for you. When you have selected a relative, write "Dialogue with [Name]" at the top of the page.

1: Assemble photographs or drawings of the person, from different stages of his or her life. In addition, gather any belongings you can—a lighter, a book, a bottle of perfume, a scarf, or anything that reminds you of the person. If you don't have photos or possessions, don't worry, just skip ahead to the next step. If you do, begin the exercise by gazing at the photos and touching the objects for a few moments. (Throughout the dialogue, you may wish to gaze back at the photos or touch the objects again.) If you wish, light a candle as you begin this exercise to symbolize this person's inner spirit. Note your thoughts and feelings as you look at the photo or handle the objects, and jot these down.

2: Make a list of all the facts you know about this person's life. Your list may be long or short. Just record what you know, such as:

Born in 1932.
Married Uncle Harold in 1950.
Worked as a seamstress for four years.
Disappeared in 1962.
Had 2 children, Lisa and Fred.
Got straight A's on high school report cards.
Had to wear braces as a child.
Huge fight with grandfather Barnes over wanting to go to college

3: Reread the list and try to put the facts in roughly chronological order. You don't need to copy them over, simply put a 1 next to the event that came first, a 2 next to the following event, etc. Don't worry if you are uncertain of dates. Do the best you can.

4: Read the events in order, beginning with the first. As you read through the chronology of your relative's life, begin to imagine yourself in the flow of these events, the inner feel of this person's unfolding life history. You may wish to close your eyes and allow images to form of your relative at different points in his or her life. Notice whatever images or emotions you become aware of as you contemplate your relative's history, and jot these down.

5: After you have read over the entire list of events and any additional notes you've made, close your eyes and imagine your relative's presence. Allow his or her image to form in your mind's eye. Once the image has formed, greet your relative in whatever way feels appropriate. Then open your eyes enough to write and begin your dialogue. Ask whatever questions you have, and record the person's answers. Allow the dialogue to flow freely.

If you get stuck, close your eyes again and focus on the image of the person in your mind's eye. Or glance back at the photos, objects, or list of life events. Be patient and don't worry about getting "right" answers. Accept whatever comes. When you have gathered as much information as you wish, thank your relative for the insights, and say good-bye in whatever way you want. You may wish to give or receive something symbolic from him or her as you say farewell. If you lit a candle, for example, you may now blow it out.

6: Read back over your dialogue, and record your thoughts and feelings, images that pass through your mind, or any additional questions you might want to ask in a future dialogue. What have you learned about yourself? about your relative? about your roles within your larger family? How has this person's life influenced you? Why do you think this particular relative "came" to you at this point in your search for self-knowledge?

BEFORE YOU TAKE THE NEXT STEP

- Have these exercises provided answers to the questions you posed in chapter 14, in **Step 1**?
- Have these exercises changed your questions?

16

Step 3: Evaluate Family Influences

The next step is to evaluate the impact of your family's work history on your career. The following four exercises enable you to apply different "lenses" to your career path. Like the different angles of refraction in eyeglasses, each exercise brings to light different types of connections between your experiences in your family and your experiences—positive and negative—in the workplace.

DETERMINE THE ROLE OF HAND-ME-DOWN DREAMS IN YOUR CAREER

The first exercise in this chapter, "Hand-Me-Down Dreams Self-Assessment," asks you to examine your current work situation, then determine the role of hand-me-down dreams in your career. You will clarify what you have gained and lost through trying to fulfill hand-me-down dreams, and what the "roads not taken" in your life have been. Reviewing **chapters 1–3** will assist you in doing this exercise.

WHAT FAMILY GHOSTS HAUNT YOUR WORKPLACE?

Exercise 16-2, "Assessing Family Influences on Relationships at Work: Authority, Teamwork, and Leadership," establishes links between what you learned about authority, leadership, and teamwork in your family and your successes and frustrations in each type of relationship at work. Recognizing these links can slow down instinctive reactions to colleagues who trigger old family patterns, and will help you to substitute new, constructive behaviors. Reviewing **chapter 13** will help you with this exercise.

DEFINE FAMILY VALUES ABOUT WORK, SUCCESS, AND MONEY

Exercise 16-3, "Defining Family Values About Work, Success, and Money," asks you to review your parents' values about these three topics. You'll clarify discrepancies between what your parents' behavior indicated they valued and what they said was important. You'll define how your values have been influenced for good or ill by your family, how you want to modify them, and how your family might respond to these changes. **Chapter 11** provides the framework for this exercise.

DEFINE THE IMPACT OF CHILDHOOD ABUSE ON YOUR CAREER

Finally, if you are a survivor of childhood abuse, the fourth exercise, 16-4, "Assessing the Impact of Abuse on Your Career Path," reviews your emotional and behavioral responses to the abuse you experienced as a child and analyzes current work relationships or situations that evoke similar responses. The goal is to break the grip of past patterns on your behavior at work. The headings in this exercise are keyed to the material covered in **chapter 10.**

Abusive relationships at their core are about distortions of trust and power. Such distortions can happen to greater or lesser degrees in any family. For that reason, even if you wouldn't describe your relationships with parents or other family members as abusive, you might benefit from reviewing the questions regarding family lessons about power, and about what can and cannot be done to talk back to or limit power.

ABOUT THE EXERCISES

As with the exercises in previous chapters, the following questions cover an enormous range of individual and family history. Don't try to answer them all at once. Your family's influence evolved over your entire lifetime. You won't find all the answers in one sitting, and if you try, you may feel overwhelmed. Take your time. Begin with the questions you're drawn to, and return to others later.

Periodically reread your answers and continue to add new insights and observations. Consult other family members for their perspectives. And trust your intuition. Remember, you aren't seeking "right" answers but answers that make sense to you and reveal themes or patterns that link your own history with your family's. Answers like that can't be rushed or forced; they emerge from a mental and emotional digestive process. Take it easy. Take it slowly. Mull. Allow the questions you need to think about to find you.

✦ ✦ ✦ ✦ ✦

EXERCISE 16-1 *Hand-Me-Down Dreams Self-Assessment*

Your Current Work

Are you happy with the work you are doing now?
If you are, how did family influences help you to find it?
If you aren't, how did you wind up in it?
How long have you known you aren't happy?
What efforts have you made to change?
How did family influences contribute to your choosing this work, and/or your continuing to do it?
Are there any aspects of your current work you want to continue doing?
What parts of your work do you want to leave behind forever?
Do you know what you would rather do?
What has blocked you from changing so far?
What is your family's attitude toward the work you'd rather do?

Hand-Me-Down Dreams

What hand-me-down dreams of your parents or grandparents have you fulfilled or tried to fulfill?
How long have you known these were hand-me-down dreams?
What kind of response did you expect from your parents or grandparents to your efforts?
What kind of response did you get?
What effect did this response have on your efforts? (gave up, tried harder, tried again, etc.)
How have you enjoyed or benefited from your efforts?
What has been difficult or disappointing about your efforts?
What were the "roads not taken" while you were fulfilling hand-me-down dreams?
Do you currently feel free to pursue your own dreams?
If yes, why? What's different now?
If not, why not?
What would have to change for you to feel free?

✦ ✦ ✦ ✦ ✦

EXERCISE 16-2 *Assessing Family Influences on Relationships at Work: Authority, Teamwork, and Leadership*

Relationships with Authority

Who has been the best or most effective boss or supervisor you've ever had?

What made him or her effective with you? (style of feedback, frequency of contact, how closely or loosely he or she monitored your work, etc.)

Who has been the worst or least effective boss or supervisor you've ever had?

What made him or her ineffective with you?

How do you respond when a boss or supervisor appreciates and rewards your work? (take pleasure in their approval, become confused or suspicious, etc.)

How do you respond when a boss or supervisor treats you unfairly? (report the person to a higher-up, start looking for your next job, assume it's your fault, ask for reasons, etc.)

What did your parents do effectively and fairly in exercising their authority over you when you were growing up?

What did your parents do ineffectively or unfairly in exercising their authority over you when you were growing up?

How did you respond to your parents' authority? (defied it, respected it, avoided it, resented it, etc.)

Why did you adopt these strategies?

In retrospect, how did the example of your parents' authority influence your expectations of authority in the workplace?

How did the strategies you used to deal with your parents' authority influence those you currently use to deal with positive and negative expressions of authority in the workplace?

What skills do you need to improve to benefit from positive uses of authority in the workplace? (accept constructive criticism, ask for help when you need it, etc.)

What skills do you need to improve to protect yourself from negative uses of authority in the workplace? (communicate your concerns clearly, set limits on destructive behavior, seek help from others, etc.)

Relationships with Teammates or Colleagues

What has been your most enjoyable or productive experience of participating on a team or collaborating on a project with colleagues?

How would you describe your own and colleagues' behavior during the collaboration?

What has been your most frustrating or least productive experience of participating on a team or collaborating on a project with colleagues?

How would you describe your own and colleagues' behavior during the collaboration?

When you were growing up, how often and on what types of projects did you and your siblings, or the family as a whole, collaborate? (dividing up household chores, cleaning up the garage, cooking a meal, decorating the house for the holidays, etc.)

What did you like or dislike about these experiences?

How were you rewarded or punished for effective or ineffective teamwork?

How would you describe your own and other family members' behavior while collaborating? (pitching in together, competing for leadership, siblings "sleazing out" of responsibilities, everybody passively waiting to be told what to do, etc.)

In retrospect, how did these early experiences with teamwork influence your expectations of collaborations at work?

What skills do you need to improve in order to participate constructively on collaborative projects? (diminish competitiveness, speak your mind, allow others to volunteer, etc.)

What skills do you need to improve in order to cope effectively when collaboration breaks down? (set limits, give clear and prompt feedback about the breakdown, ask for cooperation, etc.)

Exercising Leadership

What has been your best or most satisfying experience exercising leadership or supervising others at work?

How did you define your objectives in leading these individuals? (getting them to do what you wanted, helping them do their best, keeping employees in line, etc.)

What made these individuals satisfying to lead? (they did everything they were told, they didn't have to be told, they never bothered you, they liked you, etc.)

What has been your worst or most frustrating experience exercising leadership or supervising others at work?
How did you define your objectives in leading these individuals?
What made these individuals difficult to lead?
When you were growing up, what kinds of responsibilities did you have for managing or keeping tabs on siblings or other family members? (baby-sitting, monitoring chores, reporting on siblings' misbehavior, reporting on one parent's conduct to the other, etc.)
How did the person who assigned you this task define your objectives?
By what criteria was your supervisory performance evaluated?
How were you rewarded and/or punished for your performance?
In retrospect, what did you learn from these early experiences about the objectives of leading or supervising?
How was your leadership style influenced by these experiences? (bossy, pleading, threatening, placating, inspiring, etc.)
How were the rewards you seek at work and the punishments you dread influenced by these experiences?
How are the people you find it easy to supervise similar to or different from family members whose behavior you were responsible for in the past?
How are the people you find it difficult to supervise similar to or different from family members whose behavior you were responsible for in the past?
What skills do you need to improve to lead "difficult" individuals more effectively? (let go of need to be liked, delegate more tasks, communicate more openly, clarify consequences, etc.)
What objectives do you want your style of leadership to embody?
How close are you currently to reaching that goal?
What could you do to get closer?

✦ ✦ ✦ ✦ ✦

EXERCISE 16-3 *Defining Family Values About Work, Success, and Money*

Your Parents' Values

What do your parents' actual career decisions and their behavior tell you about the following?

- Why did or do they work?
- What does money mean?
- How did they know if they were successful?

What would your parents *say* their answers to these questions were?

How do you account for any discrepancies between their words and behavior?

Do you think your parents recognized the discrepancies? Why or why not?

How have you been affected by the discrepancies?

How similar or different are each of your parents' answers to these questions?

How have your parents dealt with any conflicts between their values about work, success, and money?

How have you been affected by these conflicts?

How have your parents' values about work, money, and success been helpful to them over the course of their lives?

How have these values been harmful or hurtful to them over the course of their lives?

Your Values

What answers do your actual career decisions and your behavior give to these same questions:

- Why do you work?
- What does money mean?
- How do you know if you're a success?

What would you have said your answers were before answering the questions above?

How do you account for any discrepancies?
How have your answers been influenced by your parents' values?
What has been helpful about these values over the course of your life?
What has been harmful or hurtful about them over the course of your life?
Do you want to change your values about work, money, or success?
How would these new values help you?
What would you have to change?
Who in your family would understand and accept your new values?
Who might have difficulty understanding or approving, and why?
How will you respond to misunderstanding or disapproval?
How might these new values benefit others in your family as well as yourself?

✦ ✦ ✦ ✦ ✦

EXERCISE 16-4 *Assessing the Impact of Abuse on Your Career*

Clarifying the Impact of Abuse

How were you abused? (verbally, sexually, emotionally, physically)

How did the person who abused you acquire and maintain power over you? (age, size, family rank, physical strength, etc.)

What did the abuse teach you to expect from people with power?

How did the person who abused you hide the abuse, prevent you from reporting it, or prevent others from finding out or stopping it? (bribes, threats, saying it was your fault, calling it "normal discipline" or "teaching," etc.)

What did you learn could and could not be done in response to abuses of power?

At the time, why did you think the abuse was happening to you?

Who did you think was responsible?

When and how did you recognize that what happened to you was abusive?

When and how did you recognize that the person who abused you was responsible for his or her actions?

Moving from Reenacting Abuse to Reinventing It

Review your past and present work situations. Have you been devalued, harassed, or mistreated by bosses or colleagues?

In what ways has the situation reenacted the abuse you experienced in the past?

How did the people involved reflect what you had learned about people with power?

How did your response reflect what you had learned about what could and could not be done in response to abuses of power?

What types of workplace behaviors that may have seemed "normal" or "familiar" in the past do you now see as abusive?

What do you currently believe you can do in response to abuses of power? (If you aren't sure what you can do, consult friends, colleagues, or others you trust for their opinions, then decide what makes sense to you.)

From whom—inside or outside work—can you seek support if someone is abusing his or her power? (If you aren't sure whom to trust, answer the next two questions.)

In the past, how did you go about deciding whom to trust? (i.e., Did you trust everyone until someone betrayed you? Did you never trust anyone because you assumed you would be betrayed?)

What criteria can you apply in deciding whom to trust, and for what can you trust them? (If you don't know what these criteria could be, ask people you respect how they decide, and try out their suggestions until you're ready to decide for yourself.)

What criteria have you used in the past to select employers, bosses, and work environments?

What criteria do you want to apply in the future? (If you aren't sure what criteria to apply, consult others for a range of opinions, then decide what makes sense to you.)

Protector, Healer, or Enforcer of Justice

To what extent has your past or current work involved you in redressing abuse? (i.e., through direct service to individuals or families or through education, health care, social policy, or legal work)

How would you describe the role you play? (protector, healer, enforcer of justice, etc.)

What is your motivation for doing this work?

How similar are the situations you encounter at work to the abuse you experienced as a child?

What is beneficial to you about doing this work?

What is difficult or draining to you about doing this work? (Try also seeking the opinion of people who care about you, and compare their answers with yours. If their answers are different, how do you account for the difference between the effects they see and what you see?)

What goals do you hope to achieve through your work?

Are these goals realistic and reasonable for an individual to attain? (Once again, ask others you respect for their opinions and compare them with your own.)

How can you reduce or alter your goals so they are realistic and reasonable? (If you don't know how, ask other people in your field how they set their goals.)

Do you set limits on the amount of time and energy you invest in your work? (Be sure to consult people who care about you for their opinions and compare them with your own answer.)

How much time do you currently invest in your personal life? (friends, family, hobbies, cultural events, etc.)

How much time do you think would be healthy to invest in your personal life? (Be sure to consult others on this and compare their opinions with your own.)

If you're currently investing less time than you think is healthy, how did you get into that pattern?

To alter the pattern, how would you alter your priorities?

What is valuable and important about you and your life separate from the work you do?

What is your Achilles' heel—the place where you forget your own pain, vulnerability, or your emotional or physical needs?

How must you learn to protect yourself from harm?

Do You Work Too Hard and Enjoy It Too Little?

Do you believe or do others consistently tell you that you work too hard, that you're a workaholic, an overachiever, or a perfectionist?

Do you feel that you are driven to work hard, as opposed to enjoying or choosing to do so?

If your answers to either of the first two questions were yes, in what ways does this situation feel familiar? In other words, how does it mirror conditions in your family when you were growing up? (work and family both feel chaotic, colleagues expect me to do everything just as my parents did, etc.)

How does your current role at work duplicate the role or "job assignment" you had when you were growing up? (staving off crises, keeping things organized, taking care of everyone, etc.)

What would have happened to your family if you had stopped performing that job?

How often did family members express gratitude, acknowledge your contributions, or say, "That's enough—take a break"?

If these things were never said, or not said often, what did you learn about your value to the family? your worth as a person? about how to gain acceptance from others? from yourself?

How do these lessons show up in your current work situation?

How do you wish your family had thanked you, acknowledged your efforts, or set limits on what they asked from you?

What difference would that have made for you in the past? today?

What would happen if you stopped working so hard?

Over time, how would others cope—and possibly benefit—if you stopped working so hard?

Over time, how would you cope—and possibly benefit—if you stopped working so hard or altogether stopped working for a time?

If you could choose a different way to live and work, what would it be? (Do not be practical or "responsible" in your answer. That side of you is overdeveloped. Try to imagine a life that would be the opposite of the one you've lived.)

What would you enjoy about that life?

How would you have to redefine your priorities or your self-worth to attain it?

How would it change you to *live* it?

Reclaiming Goals and Opportunities

Were there educational and/or career plans that you were not able to pursue because of the abuse you experienced—or the time and energy required to heal from it? (These may but don't have to be specific plans; it could be the opportunity to finish high school or attend college.)

What difference would it have made in your life if you'd been able to take advantage of these opportunities?

Have you grieved the loss of these opportunities? How?

If you haven't, what could you do to come to terms with the loss? (therapy, prayer, meditation, journal writing, self-reflection, etc.)

What did you learn from surviving abuse?

In your experience, what do other people often not understand about the impact of abuse?

What inner qualities and strengths did you have to develop in order to heal your emotional wounds?

How will these qualities and strengths benefit you in future school and/or work experiences?

What educational or career opportunities do you want to "circle back" to and take advantage of now?

What emotional resources will you need to call upon in order to attain your goals? (accepting help from others, patience with the pace of change, improving confidence and self-esteem, etc.)

Overcoming the Spiritual Wounds of Abuse

What effect did the abuse you experienced have on you spiritually? Alternatively, how did it affect your philosophy of life or worldview? (attitudes about God, love, the purpose of life, family, society, etc.)

How are your spiritual or philosophical beliefs reflected in the work you've chosen to do, or how you do it?

What beliefs sustain you?

Is your current work aligned with these beliefs? If not, how could you bring your work into alignment with them?

If you don't have beliefs that sustain you (or don't sustain you adequately), where and how could you look? (returning to the tradition you grew up with, exploring spiritual practices from other cultures, etc. If you can't think of anything, ask other people, especially other abuse survivors, where they have turned for spiritual sustenance.)

If you felt connected to a larger pattern, purpose, or meaning in life, would this change the work you do or how you did it? How?

If you imagine the abuse you experienced as an initiation into human pain and suffering, what has it prepared you to understand or to do?

Is that a challenge you are ready or willing to accept?

If not, what would have to change for you to accept it?

BEFORE YOU TAKE THE NEXT STEP

- Have these exercises provided answers to the questions you posed in **Step 1**?
- Have they changed your questions?

17

Step 4: Rediscover Your True Self

Now that you understand better how family history influenced your career decisions, it's time to compare the decisions you made as a result of family influences with career decisions you would have made for yourself and as yourself alone. To make these distinctions, you need to gather information about your *true self*.

The following exercise, "Looking for Clues to Your True Self," asks you to define the distinct individual you have always been beneath, despite, and in tandem with whoever you thought you should, could, or had to be to respond to family needs. Like an invisible twin, your individuality has always been there, even if you weren't always paying attention. You can define your true self. But you must look both backward and within to do so.

ABOUT THE EXERCISE

Do this exercise when you're feeling lighthearted and calm. Don't try doing it if you're feeling stressed or pressured about career decisions. Wait until you feel relaxed. The questions require you to use your imagination, to speculate about your "calling," and to open your mind to new possibilities. If you're anxious, you may feel pressured to nail down the answers to what you should do next. Losing patience will defeat the purpose of the exercise.

✦ ✦ ✦ ✦ ✦

EXERCISE 17-1 *Looking for Clues to Your True Self*

Childhood Play

What games or activities gave you joy as a child? (If you can't remember playing, imagine what you would have loved doing. Or watch children at play and see what types of activity attract you.)
What role would you adopt in childhood fantasy play?
What appealed to you about these types of play?
How did family members respond to this play? (Did they encourage, discourage, or ignore you?)
How was your play influenced by their responses?
How were your favorite forms of play different from those of your siblings?
What do these differences suggest about your distinct personality, interests, or talents?
What adult roles or functions did your play or fantasy role represent a child's version of?
What are the adult equivalents of this form of play?
What careers utilize the adult form of this play?
To what extent has your career utilized this type of play?
To what extent have you played in this way in your adult life outside of work?
If you haven't played in this way either at work or in your personal life, why haven't you?
If this type of play isn't already present in your work, how could you integrate it into it?
What effect would this type of play have on your work life?
If it isn't already present in your personal life, how could you integrate this type of play into it?
What effect would it have on you?

What Are You Most Afraid to Try Doing?

What are you most afraid to try doing—so much it's almost too frightening to say it aloud? (These are things you want to do, not dangerous or painful activities. The fear stems from admitting you want it, not from anticipating harm.)

What is frightening about admitting you want this?
If you tried to do this, what is the absolute *worst* thing that could happen?
How would you deal with it?
What is the *best* thing that could happen?
How would it change you?

The Example of Others

What work of another person, living or dead, do you believe you would find fulfilling to pursue? (Focus not on the product, but the process—e.g., not having written *War and Peace,* but the process of writing it.)
What would you like about the work?
If you had or could perform this work, how would it change you?
Can you imagine something similar that you could work on, either alone or with others?
What would it feel like to be engaged in such work?

Under- and Overutilized Strengths and Talents

What strengths and talents have you utilized the most in your work and your life in general? (taking charge, being empathetic, teaching, mediating, analytical problem solving, troubleshooting, etc.)
Reviewing your list, why were these particular strengths and talents important to you during this part of your life?
Ask a few people who know you well to name the strengths and talents you have utilized the most, and compare their lists with yours. What strengths and talents did you leave out? Why did you miss them?
What strengths and talents have been *underutilized* in your work and your life in general?
Reviewing your list, why have these particular strengths and talents been less important—or less accessible—to you during these years in your life?
Ask a few people who know you well to name the strengths and talents that have been underutilized in your life, and compare their lists with yours. What strengths and talents did you leave out? Why did you miss them?
Which of these underutilized strengths and talents do you feel you are being called upon to develop more fully at this point in your

life? (Not what you consciously want or think you should want but what you feel an inner force is pulling you to develop, whether you approve or not.)

Why do you think this inner force is guiding you toward these particular strengths and talents right now?

How would utilizing these strengths and talents change you?

What activities—professional and personal—would enable you to develop those strengths and talents? (Don't be practical yet. Allow your imagination to answer. If you have trouble thinking of what you could do, imagine what someone else could do.)

Moments of Purpose

List three or four moments from your past in which you have felt a deep sense of purpose—when you felt you were doing what you are meant to do or were being the person you are destined to be. Let your intuition guide you to these moments. Don't think about it too much, and don't second-guess, analyze, or judge the moments that come to mind. Look for the inner feeling of *rightness,* alignment, or unity. These moments might or might not have anything to do with work.

As you review your list, what links these moments together?

How would you summarize your role or purpose in these endeavors? (If you have trouble answering this question, imagine you are reviewing someone else's list, and define his or her role or purpose in these moments.)

How could you generalize from this evidence about what your life's purpose might be?

Imagine a future "moment of purpose" that would give you the same feeling as those from your past. What would you be doing?

Would this endeavor require you to exercise those strengths and talents you feel called upon to develop more fully? How?

Learning

What do you want to learn next in life in each of the following categories:

- Cultural or intellectual knowledge? (anthropology, folklore, math, etc.)
- Physical, artistic, or mental skills? (watercolors, skiing, computers, etc.)

• Personal qualities? (independence, honesty, tenacity, patience, etc.)

Why are you drawn to learning these things right now?
How would learning these things change you?
What specific steps can you take to attain this learning?
When can you begin?
When will you begin?
If you "will" begin later than you can begin, why would you postpone gaining knowledge you feel drawn to?

Taking Money Out of the Picture

Imagine that you have a lifetime supply of money. After all your material desires were satisfied, what would you do with the rest of your life?
In what small, specific ways can you integrate these goals or activities into your life today?

Your Definition of "Good" Work

In general, what do you believe is the greatest good anyone can do? Why?
What is the greatest good *you* can do? Why?
If the greatest good you can do is different from what "anyone" can do, why is it different?
To what extent does the work you have been or are performing involve doing the greatest good?
How does it affect you to be doing good—or not?
To what extent do you ideally want your work to involve either doing good or the greatest good?
What currently prevents you from reaching this ideal?
If you could reach it, how would it change you?
How could you begin working toward your ideal today (no matter what your current work situation)?
How would it change you to begin working toward your ideal degree of good work?

The Meaning of Work

If you were given the power to change today's work world to make it healthier and happier—however you define these—what would you do? Why?

Can you imagine ways to integrate any of these changes into your own life now? How?

If you were asked to pass on the wisdom you've gained about work from your own career to the next generation, what would you teach them to seek and to avoid?

Are you currently seeking and avoiding those things yourself? If you are, how? If you aren't, why aren't you?

Putting the Clues Together

After reviewing your answers in this exercise, what have you learned about your true self?

Did anything surprise you?

Did anything dismay or frighten you?

Did anything make you happy?

To what extent has the career you've had been a good fit for the person profiled above?

To what extent has the career you've had been mismatched to the person profiled above?

What are the possibilities opening before you at this point in your life?

What are the dangers or pitfalls you are confronting at this point in your life?

How is the "true self" profiled above similar to and different from the person your family believes you to be?

What career would you design for the person profiled above if you were starting from scratch? Why?

BEFORE YOU TAKE THE NEXT STEP

- Have these exercises provided answers to the questions you posed in **Step 1**?
- Have they changed your questions?

18

Step 5: Name What You Want

Once you've defined your true self, you need to find ways to express it. This step asks you to generate ideas about types of work or areas of interest that are good bets to fit your needs. The exercise, "Identifying Work That Fits," asks you to come up with a list of types of work that match your purpose, talents, and goals for learning; to gather specific information about the field; to evaluate and summarize your findings; and then to name what you want.

ABOUT THE EXERCISE

You should answer these questions in order. Each question provides important information you will need to respond to in later questions. You may be tempted to skip immediately from brainstorming to action planning. But like leaping from a first date to the altar, it's a bad idea for similar reasons. Your fantasies may not fit the realities revealed over time.

During this exercise, be alert to two dangers. They are likely to arise now because you are closing in on your goals. Like wind across a desert stirring up a sandstorm, the prospect of change may kick up old, habitual fears and doubts. But you can take precautions to minimize the dangers.

IF YOU'RE DRAGGING YOUR FEET, BOOST YOUR CONFIDENCE

The first danger in naming what you want is that you generate ideas, then drag your feet about gathering information about them. You may be afraid that the data you gather will dampen your enthusiasm. It may seem preferable to hang on to a dream, even an unrealistic one, than to be forced by hard facts to give it up. At least you still have a dream.

The source of this fear is usually lack of confidence in your ability to overcome barriers to transforming dreams into plans, plans into realities. You can overcome almost any obstacle as long as you patiently study it and line up the resources you need to move ahead. The exercise that follows in **Step 6** will help you identify resources to change effectively.

Remember, too, that the only way you clear the path toward the things you do want is by brushing away the things you thought you wanted but discover you either didn't want or can't attain. Dreams should mobilize energy, not gum it up. Dreams become illusions when you cling to them after it's clear they will never intersect with reality. You have to let them go. Doing so is the only way to find the dreams you *can* pursue.

IF YOU FEEL LIKE GIVING UP, FIND OUT WHY

The other danger in naming what you want is becoming overwhelmed by the amount of effort it takes to gather information, then giving up out of exhaustion or discouragement. What's helpful at these times is to find out why you're getting stuck.

• **When you're trying to brainstorm ideas, do you go blank, then give up?** If so, you need to find an external resource to "reboot" your mind. Ask a friend or colleague for input. Look at some books or magazines. Or do something physical or sensual to relax, then return to the question later.

• **Do you try to answer too many questions at once, and then feel exhausted and stressed?** If so, pace yourself. Defining what you want in life is a long-distance run, not a sprint. The only person you're competing with is yourself. You'll get more done in the long haul by discovering your natural stride and taking breaks than by running flat out from the starting line. Some of your best ideas are likely to arise when you're not directly thinking about the questions.

• **Do you compare yourself to experts in the field and think, "I could never get there. I might as well not start"?** If so, remember that everybody is a beginner at some point. People attain expertise step by step. You can, too. Others have gotten where you want to be before you, not because they were born there, but because they kept walking until they arrived. If you invest time and effort, you can walk there, too.

Being stuck is not who you are, it's a temporary experience you can learn from and leave behind. Understanding how you get stuck reveals the solvent you need to get free.

✦ ✦ ✦ ✦ ✦

EXERCISE 18-1 *Identifying Work That Fits You*

Brainstorming

Review your answers to **Exercise 17-1** in **Step 4,** then list ten different projects, interests, or kinds of work that fit

- the strengths and talents you feel called to develop next.
- the kinds of experiences that give you a sense of purpose.
- what you want to learn next.
- your ideals for doing good.

Your list may include completely new career options; a shift of responsibilities within your current field; a service, product, or knowledge area you want to develop; or a skill you want to learn or improve.

Gathering Information

Narrow your list down to two or three items that you feel most drawn to learn more about.

Do you know (check only those you're sure of):
__ How long it takes to get started in this field or endeavor?
__ What kinds of training are usually required?
__ The expense of training or start-up costs?

Can you define:
__ The competencies required to do this work?
__ The competencies you already have?
__ The gaps you will need to fill in?

For people who enjoy and/or excel in this work, what are the typical kinds of:
__ Motivations?
__ Rewards?
__ Values?
__ Personality traits?

Do you know anyone who:
___ Is in training for or beginning this type of endeavor?
___ Has one or two years of experience?
___ Has several years of experience?
___ Left the field to begin something else?
___ Does it for love, not for money?

Do you know the industry, profession, or field's:
___ Journals or newsletters?
___ Trade, professional, or academic associations?
___ Networking associations?
___ Licensing or regulatory agencies?

Do you know what range of income you can expect:
___ As a beginner?
___ After two years?
___ After five to ten years?
___ As a freelancer or self-employed consultant?

Do you know if there are opportunities to gain experience and contacts within this field through:
___ Internships?
___ Volunteer work?
___ Part-time jobs?

Your goal is to gather as much information as you can about the field. Information interviews with people who have current or past experience are especially helpful in clarifying the "fit" between your hopes and dreams and the realities you'll encounter in this work. If you don't currently know anyone engaged in this work, your alumni association or the career center at your college or university may be able to help you locate appropriate contacts in your area. Be sure to ask each person you talk to for the names of other potential contacts.

The following resources can also help you:
Reference librarians
Professional journals or newsletters
Trade associations (most have Internet websites)
Conferences and job fairs
Networking contacts

Career counselors or coaches
Admissions offices

Reviewing Your Data

Review the information you've compiled for each of the two or three areas you listed. For each:

What information did you find discouraging? Why?
What steps could you take to overcome discouragement?
Are you currently excited or committed enough to this endeavor to take those steps? Why or why not?
What would have to change for you to be committed enough to take them?
What information did you find encouraging? Why?
Do you still consider this endeavor a good fit for you? Why or why not?
Does one of them now seem like the best fit? Why?
If the first two or three do not seem like a good fit, pick out the next most likely two or three listed items and gather information about each of them. If necessary, continue narrowing down your list until you have identified the single best match from your list. What is it? Why does it fit you best?

Name Your Goal

Now that you've identified the best fit, you must state your goal. What do you want to do with this knowledge? At this point, focus on honestly naming your desire; don't worry yet about a plan or a timeline to achieve it (you'll work on planning in **Step 7**).

What do you want?
What did you feel when you wrote down what you wanted?
What were the first thoughts that passed through your mind?
How are these feelings and thoughts similar to or different from what you expected?

BEFORE YOU TAKE THE NEXT STEP

- Have these exercises provided answers to the questions you posed in **Step 1**?
- Have they changed your questions?

19

Step 6: Identify and Overcome Barriers to Change

Now that you've named what you want, the next logical step might seem to be developing an action plan to get it. That is, in fact, what you'll do in **Step 7.** This intermediate step, however, will help prevent you from getting lost or stuck in achieving your goals. Initiating a plan of action means introducing changes—some predictable, others unpredictable—into every aspect of your life. To cope constructively with change, you need to understand your fears and vulnerabilities as well as your strengths and resources. The following exercises enable you to anticipate stumbling blocks, and to navigate smoothly around them.

The first exercise, "Exploring Your Relationship with Change," asks you to define your family's beliefs about change; to review past changes you managed successfully; and to learn from past changes that didn't turn out as you wanted. You'll outline potential barriers to change and the resources to overcome them—both inner and outer.

Exercise 19-2, "Predicting Your Future History," helps you to synthesize the information you've gathered about your approach to change. You'll imagine yourself at a date after you've achieved your current goal, then you'll tell the story of how you got there. This "rehearsal" forces you to visualize the outcome you're striving for and to imagine yourself already having overcome all obstacles to your goal.

ABOUT THE EXERCISES

As with previous exercises, you may find yourself drawn to some questions more than others. Follow your instincts. You can always return to the other questions later. But try to answer enough of the questions so that you can predict the fears, doubts, and negative expectations that might get in your way, and to identify resources that will enable you to advance toward your goal. Review **chapter 12** before you begin the exercises.

✦ ✦ ✦ ✦ ✦

Exercise 19-1 *Exploring Your Relationship with Change*

Your Family's Experience with Change

What were some major changes your family went through when you were growing up? (moving to a new place, a parent losing a job, a sibling leaving home for college, etc.)

How did different family members behave in response to these changes? (talked more/less, fought more, change in sense of humor or playfulness, weight gain/loss, greater or lesser time with family, etc.)

What did their behavior (both positive and negative) suggest they felt about the changes?

What did they say about the changes? ("Change is exciting"; "Change is dangerous"; "Change is horrible but necessary"; "Change brings opportunity"; etc.)

Did what they said about change differ from what their behavior suggested they felt?

At the time, how did you respond to these mixed messages?

In retrospect, what strikes you as healthy and constructive in the way different family members coped with change?

What strikes you as ineffective or problematic in the way different family members coped with change?

What did you learn about change from your family's example?

Your Experience with Change

What are some major changes you've experienced as an adult?

What has been healthy and constructive in your response to these changes?

What has been ineffective or problematic in your response to these changes?

Identifying a Successful Change

What is one major, positive change you successfully achieved?

Study that change as you would a historical event:

- Who initiated the change?
- What steps preceded the change?

- How did you plan it?
- Who helped you? How and why?
- Who hindered you? How and why?
- What happened as you expected it would?
- What surprised you?
- What attitudes helped you to succeed?
- What obstacles got in your way?
- How did you overcome them?
- How did changing successfully make you feel?
- How did the change affect your future?
- What did you learn about yourself?
- How can you apply what you learned to planning current changes?

Identifying a Change You Weren't Able to Make

What is one major change you wanted but weren't able to make? Study that change as you would a historical event:

- Who initiated the change?
- What steps preceded the change?
- How did you plan it?
- Who helped you? Why?
- Who hindered you? Why?
- What happened as you expected it would?
- What surprised you?
- When and how did your efforts to change stall or break down?
- What were the warning signs?
- How did you respond to them?
- What obstacles got in your way?
- What prevented you from overcoming them?
- What attitudes, expectations, doubts, or fears got in your way?
- In retrospect, what would you do differently today?
- How did you feel about not doing what you wanted?
- How did this outcome affect your future?
- What did you learn about yourself?
- How can you apply what you learned to planning current changes?

Identifying Barriers and Resources

Based on past experience, what characteristic inner barriers to change do you need to watch out for? (unrealistic expectations, become easily discouraged, impatience, etc.)

What qualities do you need to develop in order to overcome these barriers? (pragmatism, patience, tenacity, etc.)

How can you begin right now to develop these qualities in your daily life?

What characteristic external barriers do you need to watch out for? (not budgeting enough time or money to complete a project, not receiving enough support from family or friends, etc.)

What resources do you need to line up in order to overcome these barriers? (borrow money, take time off from work, arrange for child care, etc.)

Who is likely to feel threatened, angry, or hurt by the changes you want to make?

What might they do to undermine your efforts?

What steps can you take to gain their support or neutralize their opposition?

Who could help you deal with them?

Who is most likely to understand and support the changes you want to make?

What kind of help can you ask them for?

Inspiration and Example

Among your family and friends, who has had to overcome adversity to achieve their goals?

What kept them strong, committed, and energetic?

What past or present public figures do you admire? Why?

What obstacles did they have to overcome to achieve their goals? How did they overcome them? (If you don't know, find a biography and read it with this question in mind.)

What lessons can you draw from their experiences to help you achieve your goals?

✦ ✦ ✦ ✦ ✦

EXERCISE 19-2 *Predicting Your Future History*

Imagine that you have time-traveled to a point in the future when the changes you currently want to make have already been completed for some time. Looking backward from the future, tell the story of how you made these changes. What barriers did you overcome? What effect did these changes have on your life? What further changes did they lead to?

BEFORE YOU TAKE THE NEXT STEP

- Have these exercises provided answers to the questions you posed in **Step 1**?
- Have they changed your questions?

20

Step 7: Make Realistic Plans

Many people assume that career planning begins with an action plan, and therefore approach it with trepidation or dread because they aren't yet sure of their goals. They therefore avoid thinking about the direction their careers are taking them (instead of the other way around) until extreme dissatisfaction forces them to pay attention. If you force yourself to make a plan before you're ready, you may find it hard to stick with it.

Making plans, however, can be the most straightforward and exciting part of career planning. If you've done enough inward soul searching and outward information gathering before you begin, you'll know what you want, what you can get, and what you can do to get it. You can then generate tangible but flexible plans—and follow them with optimism and confidence.

YOU'VE DONE THE HARDEST WORK ALREADY

If you've completed the first six steps, you've already done the hardest work. The following exercise, "Planning for Change," asks you to translate the knowledge you've gained into a plan that brings your everyday life into accord with who you are. Even if you aren't changing careers—you may simply want to work less, retool your current job, learn French, resume playing the piano, or become a Buddhist—you'll still benefit from making a plan.

WHAT A PLAN WILL DO FOR YOU

A good plan doesn't have to be lengthy and shouldn't be permanent. All it has to do is provide a time frame, a "compass" to guide your activity, and a means of tracking how you're doing. These features enable you to monitor your commitment and progress toward your goal. You can celebrate small victories along the way. Or, if it turns out that your goal isn't possible—or that you don't really want it—you'll find out as soon as possible and can substitute another.

ABOUT THE EXERCISE

This exercise calls for you to establish your overall goal and to map out the short-term and long-term steps you will need to take to attain it. Don't worry if you don't know what all the steps are. At the starting point, it's unlikely that you would, which is why you should incorporate learning into your plan.

The purpose of translating your goal into a step-by-step timeline is not to tie you down but to help you predict what you'll need to keep moving forward. The hiker who starts with a packing list doesn't have to reverse course halfway up the mountain to fetch sunscreen and water.

Try to answer the questions in order. If you can't, answer as many of them as you can. Take breaks. Planning doesn't have to be odious, but it does require concentration. You'll probably get tired. Read a novel or take a bath, but don't stop planning. If you become frustrated or discouraged, the problem may not be with the plan, but with the way you treat yourself! So be gentle and patient, and loyal to your best friend in change: your plan.

Before you begin, review your answers to the exercises in **Steps 4** and **5**, especially the goal you named at the end of **Exercise 18-1,** "Identifying Work That Fits You."

✦ ✦ ✦ ✦ ✦

EXERCISE 20-1 *Planning for Change*

Establish Your Goals

Based on everything you learned about yourself in **Steps 1–6**, what is your goal—or goals—for change?

How will you know you've achieved your goal?

When do you want to complete it?

Give each goal you've listed a reality check. Is there a goal that should come first? (If you've written "Become a psychotherapist," do you have any experience with counseling? If not, your preliminary goal should be, "Find out if I like counseling.")

What are your revised goals?

Commit Your Time

When will you begin?

What do you need to finish before you begin?

What resources do you need to line up before you begin? (Consult your answers to **Exercise 19-1.**)

How much time per week will you set aside for each goal?

Review the completion date you set. Is this enough time per week?

If it's not, increase your hours per week if you can, or if you can't, extend your completion date into the future.

How will you protect this time every week? (hire a baby-sitter, write in your calendar, don't answer the phone, etc.)

Short-Term Timeline

For each goal, list small specific actions you will take to reach it. Include an estimate of the amount of time you think each step will take and a place to check off each activity as you complete it.

- This week:
- This month:
- Over the next six months:

Long-Term Timeline

For each goal, list projects you will complete over longer spans of time. These will be broader actions—the cumulative effects of small steps—than those in your short-term timeline (e.g., "Complete first-year of MBA degree," instead of "Fill out application to graduate school").

- This year:
- Over the next two years:
- Over the next five years:

Review and Update Your Plan

Mark periodic dates on your calendar to review your progress. If you can, review your plan at least once a month.
What steps did you complete?
How can you reward or congratulate yourself for these achievements?
What steps didn't you complete?
What prevented you from completing them?
What can you do to avoid similar difficulties in the future?
How accurate were your estimates of the amount of time each step would take?
If you tend to overestimate or underestimate, do you need to revise other estimates up or down?
Do you need to break any steps into smaller pieces?
What did you learn in the past month?
Do you need to modify your goals or your plan accordingly?

NOW THAT YOU'VE TAKEN THE LAST STEP (FOR NOW)

Completing your plan is only the last step in your *current* cycle of change. After you achieve your goals, you're bound to want new ones. When you do, you can go through these seven steps again. You're likely to come up with different answers—and equally valid ones—each time you do these exercises. It's amazing how history changes as we do—and so does the truth about ourselves.

So, for the last time . . .

- Have these exercises provided answers to the questions you posed in **Step 1**?
- Have they changed your questions?

Part Five

LOOKING AHEAD

✦

21

Helping Your Children to Follow Their Dreams

This chapter may not be what you expect. It's not about finding career books for your children or about tutoring, or school-to-job training programs, or even heart-to-heart talks about the family's work history. These resources can educate your children about career options. But resources alone won't prepare your children to follow their dreams—**not if you haven't first defined and made the effort to follow your own.**

The strongest psychological influence on children is what Carl Jung called the "unlived life" of their parents. To ensure that your children are free to live their own lives rather than your "unlived" one, apply everything you've learned from this book to the three tasks that follow.

1. IDENTIFY YOUR "UNLIVED" LIFE

You already know what it is. It isn't that hard to find. It's wherever you go in fantasy every time you think "What if . . ." or "I wish . . ." or "Someday . . ." If you aren't sure of the details, the exercises in **Part Four** of this book can help you refine them. Problems arise when you think of your unlived life as a fantasy, not as a serious goal for change. If you treat it as merely a fantasy, your example teaches your children to treat their greatest dreams as fantasies, too, rather than blueprints for living. Remember, to children, example is *everything.*

2. BEGIN TO LIVE YOUR "UNLIVED" LIFE

It's not a secret fantasy anymore. Once you've gone public—even if it's only with yourself—you can no longer pretend you don't care. You have to begin in some small but immediate way to live your "unlived" life. If you don't know how to begin, **Exercise 20-1** will help you develop a realistic, step-by-step plan.

As soon as you begin to grapple with your unlived life, you instantly transform it into your *lived life.* You claim responsibility for it, and you release your children from assuming the burden. You don't have to live it gracefully, quickly, smoothly, or efficiently. You don't have to do it all the time. You don't have to be the best. You don't have to be "successful" or make money. All you have to do—all your children have to see you do—is try. Outcome isn't important; effort is.

Your effort demonstrates that you take yourself seriously. It shows that change can begin at any stage of life; that barriers can be overcome; that it's important to find purpose and fulfillment; and that learning what's important to you and trying to express it matters more than pleasing other people. If your children learn these values from your example, they will be equipped with the resources and stamina they need to find and follow their own dreams.

Acts of Acceptance and Forgiveness

The following acts of acceptance and forgiveness clear the way for you to transform your unlived life from a fantasy into a goal.

- Stop trying to live your parents' unlived lives. Accept that you never could, can't now, and never will be able to.
- Forgive yourself for whatever ways you tried to but couldn't fulfill your parents' expectations. So what if you didn't earn a 4.0 average, write the great American novel, make a billion bucks, become a star quarterback, or produce grandchildren. It only matters if these goals mattered to you.
- Believe in your individuality. You aren't and never have been an emotional or psychic appendage of your parents, an extra part that slipped away. Your past, present, and future job is to be yourself.

Avoid Discouragement and Delay

Be alert to the danger of inertia. If you've spent years treating dreams as fantasies, you'll be tempted to revert to that habit. Here are three common pitfalls to avoid.

Do Not Say, "It's Too Late."

It's never too late to begin anything if you focus on enjoying and learning from what you're doing rather than an outcome or product.

Do Not Say, "I'll Get Around to It Later."

Like a fairy-tale prince turning back into a frog, this thought transforms goals for change back into wishful fantasies.

Do Not Use Your Children as a Reason Not to Try.

Small, incremental steps toward your goal will not require you to abandon your responsibilities as a parent or partner. Again, effort is what counts, not outcome. If you use your children or family duties as an excuse for giving up your dreams, your example teaches your children to equate love with sacrifice. Remember, sacrifice is not the same as giving or acting responsibly. It yields rage and resentment, not trust and gratitude.

3. WHAT YOU CAN'T LIVE, YOU MUST GRIEVE

Although it's never too late to begin anything, it can be too late to begin young. The opportunity to pursue goals that require peak physical form or body conditioning and skills training from early childhood, such as ballet, classical music, or athletics, may have passed you by. This doesn't mean you can't include these activities in your life in some form, but it won't be the same as if you'd started younger.

Whatever your goal, you have to start sometime. Whenever you start, it's not going to change that you didn't start earlier. That doesn't have to and shouldn't stop you from beginning, but it does mean you must acknowledge and grieve the time you lost. The things you wished for but never had are losses and must be mourned—just as much as things you had and lost. Our emotions don't register a distinction between imagination and reality. They respond seriously and intensely to both.

How Grief Liberates You

The purpose of grieving is not to get stuck in remorse or regret, but to ensure that you don't. If you don't admit and express your emotions, the sadness won't disappear. Your children will detect it and try to heal it. If you do confront loss, you transfer your unlived life into the afterlife. Fantasies of "what if" or "someday" can no longer taunt you with tantalizing but unreal potential, nor can they falsely reassure you that you have a plan and purpose you simply haven't gotten around to yet.

The benefit of sending truly "dead" dreams to the "afterlife" is that it liberates you to devote time and energy to what's possible and real in the present. Grief is painful and time-consuming, but it also clears away losses that otherwise "gum up" your heart and occlude your vision of choices available to you. Instead of remaining trapped in speculation about "what might be," it forces you to answer the question, "What can I do now?"

What Your Healing Teaches Children

Your willingness to grieve will eventually heal you. Your children will see that you're able to take care of yourself, leaving them free to live their own lives rather than your unlived one. Your example will teach them to have

- The courage and honesty to confront losses.
- The resilience to move beyond loss and start over.
- The wisdom to focus on the present and the possible.

Your children will learn persistence, optimism, and faith in their power to change. These substantial gifts will enable them to grow emotionally hearty and thrive—no matter what. They will be prepared not just to follow their dreams, but to respond with strength and resilience to every challenge they encounter throughout their lives.

22

The Future

This book has focused on helping you to get in touch with your dreams and desires by distinguishing them from those you inherited from your family. It has also aimed at helping you to design a career path in accord with that knowledge. Your individual quest, of course, takes shape within the broader context of society—specifically the current condition of the economy and trends within the labor market.

You have been encouraged to understand how you define success, what gives you satisfaction at work, and the skills you need to work effectively with colleagues. These insights provide resources you will need to succeed in a work environment that requires increasing amounts of self-determination, self-knowledge, and the ability to collaborate with many different types of people. Let's review the changing demands of today's work world, and summarize how they will affect your career.

HOW WORK IS CHANGING

The world of work has changed dramatically within the past decade, and the pace of change shows no signs of slacking. The shift from an industrial to a service and information-based economy has resulted in:

• The globalization of national economies and the redistribution of jobs around the world.

- A growing need for lifelong learning to keep pace with constant technological advances.
- The disappearance of some careers (e.g., much middle management) and the birth of others (e.g., website developers and genetic engineers).
- The growth of corporate downsizing and mergers.
- The disappearance of lifetime job security, even for highly skilled technical and professional workers.
- The flattening of pyramid-shaped organizational structures into matrix and team-oriented ones.
- The disappearance of traditional career ladders.
- The need to prepare for frequent shifts in employers and for several different careers over the course of a lifetime.

WHY THESE TRENDS MATTER TO YOU

If you haven't yet been affected by these seismic shifts in the working terrain, the odds are you will be. Many people have been caught unprepared for forced changes in employment or the disappearance of a career path they thought a sure bet for steady employment leading to a secure retirement. They are unprepared for change and feel angry, disappointed, or bitter that expectations for a steady climb up the career ladder will not be met—at least not in the way they'd counted on. And not in the way their parents and grandparents may have climbed it.

Understanding these trends can prevent you from being blindsided by shifts in the economy. You'll be better prepared to take charge of your career development. You'll be able to match your career goals with the current labor market. And, if you've tried to duplicate your parents' or grandparents' careers, these trends clarify why career paths that worked in the past cannot be duplicated today. In other words, even if you wanted to devote your career to fulfilling your family's hand-me-down dreams, the economy probably won't let you. As troubling as this news may be, it also frees you to find your own way.

THE OLD CONTRACT AND THE NEW PARADIGM

As pressures for profitability and competition have intensified among corporations, organizations strive to cut costs at *any* cost.

Employees suffer the brunt of these efforts. The "old contract"—to use author David Noer's term—that binds employers and employees has broken down.

What's Gone

Under the old contract, employees expected the following from employers.

- Your job title placed you within a pyramid-shaped hierarchy. Your formal job description spelled out the work you would do until or unless your job title changed.
- You would keep your job as long as you did it well, and you could expect promotions and raises based on the merits of your work.
- Loyalty from you meant making decisions based on your employer's best interests; loyalty from your employer meant rewarding you for sticking with the company by providing job security, opportunities to advance, and employee benefits.
- In return for long-term service, you could depend upon your employer for retirement planning; health and disability insurance; vacation and sick leave; and professional training to update your skills.

What's Taken Its Place

The new paradigm predicted by many business forecasters is that of the jobless future. Don't worry, it doesn't mean unemployment. There will be work and income, but they won't be structured as they were with traditional jobs in the past. The new guidelines include:

- As your employer's products and services evolve to give them a competitive edge in the marketplace, your work will change, too. Instead of having a fixed job title and description, you will work on projects with cross-functional teams. You'll have to get used to changing roles, shifting tasks, and collaborating with others.
- Work will be contingent upon your employer's current needs. You must think of them as your customers who will contract for your services and skills based upon their present needs. Your reward for good work will be renewed contracts and referrals to other customers.
- Loyalty will mean providing high-quality service, as contracted for by your employer/customer. You generate customer loyalty by

understanding what they need and providing it. They express loyalty by fulfilling contracts with you in a timely and honest way.

- You will have to learn to think of yourself as self-employed, or as the head of your own business of one—meaning you take charge of what employers used to: retirement planning; career development; negotiating fees; updating your skills; forecasting trends in your industry; and adapting your menu of products and services to stay competitive.

It sounds like a lot of work and a lot of responsibility—and it is. But the benefit of these new guidelines is that you are less dependent on the vicissitudes of any single employer, and are less vulnerable to sudden organizational changes you cannot predict or control.

Because it requires so much work, career planning within this new work environment forces you to go deeply inward to discover the passions and rewards that will motivate you to invest the necessary time and effort. The increased self-knowledge you have gained by reading this book should help you develop a career plan you can pursue with a high level of tenacity and passion—and an equally high level of rewards.

WHAT IF YOUR CAREER LOOKED LIKE THIS . . .

Managing your career is a lifelong enterprise. You can expect to fine-tune career plans over the course of a lifetime. As you do, here are some questions to help you invent your own new paradigm to make work more humane and satisfying.

What If . . . ?

- You viewed your career path as a *learning curve* in which each job was valued for the knowledge you gained, and you selected each new job because it could teach you what you wanted to learn next?
- You received recognition for your work based on how meaningful and satisfying you found it to be, and how useful it was to yourself and others?
- You adjusted the amount of time you worked, the place you worked, and the type of work you performed to fit your own and your family's changing stages of development?

• You measured success not by your title, salary, or material possessions, but by the wisdom and pleasure you have created in your life—through work, relationships, and other pursuits?

• Instead of postponing freedom and leisure until retirement, you balanced freedom and obligation, work and play in your everyday life right now?

THE DREAM AT THE CORE OF HAND-ME-DOWN DREAMS

Every time you invent new ways to make your own work more humane and satisfying, you also benefit your family and society at large. Social changes begin, after all, as individual yearnings for change. Gradually, the yearning becomes a repetitive dream. Many will say the dream is impossible. Some may say it's bad. Eventually, someone will go ahead and do it anyway. Gradually, the dream no longer seems frightening or impossible, but necessary and inevitable. It isn't a dream anymore, it's the way things are.

If there is a constant in life, it is the evolution of dreams, handed down from one generation to the next. If you crack through the surface of every family's hand-me-down dreams, you will find a single, unifying dream at their core—the dream of a happy life. The art of finding it, however, is to remember that while the dream of happiness is passed on through families, *the experience of happiness is sublimely individual.* You must build your own. This may seem frightening or impossible, but if you persevere, it will become necessary and inevitable. It won't be a dream anymore, it's the way **you** are.

APPENDIXES

✦

Appendix 1: How and When to Seek Professional Support

WHEN TO CONSULT A CAREER PROFESSIONAL

You may want to consult a career professional if you change best when working with someone else; you've tried other resources and still don't know what you want; you need a nudge; you need help in matching your skills with appropriate careers or industries; or you need guidance in deciding among different career options.

Career counselors and coaches offer expertise in some or all of these areas:

- Self-assessment inventories and personality types
- Knowledge about specific industries and labor trends
- Networking strategies
- Résumé writing and interviewing skills
- Job-hunting strategies
- Salary negotiation
- Defining competencies and skills
- Managing career transitions
- Knowledge of computer and library resources
- Matching personal goals with career opportunities

Counselors can also offer encouragement, structure, and inspiration. Career planning and job hunting are demanding. Never underestimate the benefits of enlisting someone else's cheerful optimism in the face of your own stress, self-doubt, or tiredness.

To find a career professional, ask for referrals from friends or colleagues. You may qualify for career guidance from the college or university you graduated from or you can ask the school's career office for a referral. Check the listings of your community adult education program for career workshops, since the instructors may also work with individual clients. See if your company's employee assistance program offers referrals to career counselors. If you've been downsized or laid off, find out if outplacement or career counseling are part of your exit deal, or ask for it to be included. Also, check the Yellow Pages for career resources in your area.

During your initial phone contact or your first meeting, you should feel free to ask a prospective counselor or coach about his or her training, years of experience, professional affiliations, and areas of expertise. You can also briefly describe the goals you want to work on, and ask how the counselor usually works with people who have similar goals. Your aim is to determine if the counselor has the knowledge you need and a personal and professional style you're comfortable with. You should feel free to call or interview several people to find the best fit for your needs. Don't forget to discuss hourly fees prior to your first visit.

WHEN TO CONSULT A PSYCHOTHERAPIST

You may want to consult a psychotherapist if you want to explore your emotional response to your family history; improve family relationships; or resolve hurtful memories or current familial problems. Consulting a therapist can also help if your career situation has led to emotional difficulties such as depression, hopelessness, chronic anger or anxiety, or abuse of alcohol or drugs. Don't wait until these feelings are intense. If you catch them early on, you can avert troubling extremes and can reinvest your energy into positive plans for your future.

Consulting a therapist doesn't mean there's anything wrong with you. People hire therapists to help them deal effectively with widely shared challenges. Usually, they want to understand themselves better; feel more confident and independent; or learn effective ways to communicate or cope with stress. Consulting a therapist also doesn't mean you're weak. It means you're brave enough to explore the truth about yourself and your family. Therapy doesn't have to take a long time. It can be short-term and focused on finding workable solutions to problems.

If you have a childhood abuse history and you've never consulted a therapist, you may want to do so now, especially if you're seeking a change in your career. Therapy is very effective in resolving the effects of abuse, and can help ensure that its legacy does not follow you into future career moves. If you have been in therapy before and find the readings and exercises in this book trigger painful memories, you may want to consider resuming therapy to talk through your responses.

To find a psychotherapist, ask for suggestions from friends, ministers, physicians, hospital social service departments, college or university counseling centers, or your company's employee assistance program. Your local or state government's department of mental health may also offer counseling services, or be able to make referrals. If you plan to use your health insurance, call your plan's customer service representative ahead of time to find out what your yearly outpatient mental health benefits are and whether they will cover the costs of any therapist you choose, or only "in-plan" providers. If they restrict coverage to in-plan providers, they should give you a list of those available in your area.

Psychotherapists may be social workers, psychologists, marriage and family counselors, or psychiatrists. Professionals from each discipline are licensed at different levels, according to state laws. Therapists usually specialize in one or more different types of therapy, such as cognitive and behavioral therapy, insight-oriented or psychodynamic therapy, family therapy, hypnotherapy, or mind-body approaches, to name just a few. Only psychiatrists, who are physicians, can prescribe psychopharmacological drugs.

You should feel free to ask prospective therapists what discipline they were trained in; what types of therapy they specialize in; what kind of license they have; and how many years they have been in practice. You can also briefly describe the goals you want to work toward, and ask how they usually work with clients who have similar goals. Remember to discuss fees prior to your first office visit. Feel free to interview different therapists until you find someone whose skills and knowledge you feel confident in, and with whom you feel rapport and trust.

[illegible]

[illegible]

[illegible]

Appendix 2: Recommended Reading

CAREER PLANNING AND SELF-ASSESSMENT

The following books all provide useful self-assessment exercises, advice, encouragement, information, and inspirational examples to help you clarify your unique talents and passions and find practical ways to integrate these with your career.

Do What You Love and the Money Will Follow by Marsha Sinetar (New York: Dell, 1987).

I Could Do Anything If Only I Knew What It Was: How to Discover What You Really Want and How to Get It by Barbara Sher (New York: Delacorte, 1994).

To Build the Life You Want, Create the Work You Love by Marsha Sinetar (New York: St. Martin's Griffin, 1996).

The Complete Job-Search Handbook: All the Skills You Need to Get Any Job and Have a Good Time Doing It by Howard Figler (New York: Holt, 1988).

What Color Is Your Parachute? A Practical Manual for Job-Hunters and Career Changers by Richard Bolles (Berkeley, Calif.: Ten Speed Press, 1991).

Wishcraft: How to Get What You Really Want by Barbara Sher (New York: Ballantine, 1983).

Zen and the Art of Making a Living: A Practical Guide to Creative Career Design by Laurence Boldt (New York: Penguin Arkana, 1993).

FAMILY RELATIONSHIPS

The following two books by Harriet Lerner bring the depth and richness of family systems theory to bear on intimate relationships, with great compassion and practicality. These are both user-friendly books that can help you understand how relationships break down and how to get them back on track.

The Dance of Anger: A Woman's Guide to Changing the Patterns of Intimate Relationships by Harriet Goldhor Lerner (New York: Harper & Row, 1985).
The Dance of Intimacy: A Woman's Guide to Courageous Acts of Change in Key Relationships by Harriet Goldhor Lerner (New York: Harper, 1989).

If you want to understand the nature of sibling relationships and parents' influence upon them, this book is very informative. It's well researched and written in an accessible style.

The Sibling Bond by Stephen P. Bank and Michael D. Kahn (New York: Basic Books, 1982).

This book explores intergenerational family connections, presents in-depth case studies of well-known families, and offers constructive suggestions on ways to improve and heal your relationships with your family.

You Can Go Home Again: Reconnecting with Your Family by Monica McGoldrick (New York: Norton, 1995).

COPING WITH JOB LOSS

If you're exploring career options because you were laid off or your company was downsized, these books provide encouragement, information, and advice on keeping your spirits high while planning your next career move. Cliff Hakim's book is written like a novel, following the story of one person through the different stages of transition. Its description of networking is especially useful. William Byron's book is aimed at midcareer job loss and is imbued with a spiritual perspective.

When You Lose Your Job: Laid Off, Fired, Early Retired, Relocated, Demoted, Unchallenged by Cliff Hakim (San Francisco: Berrett-Koehler, 1993).
Finding Work Without Losing Heart: Bouncing Back from Mid-Career Job Loss by William J. Byron (Holbrook, Mass.: Adams, 1995).

INTERNET RESOURCES

If you have access to the Internet, career resources are abundant and growing. If you don't have your own computer, check your community library; many offer Internet access to patrons.

Job-Hunting on the Internet by Richard Bolles (Berkeley, Calif.: Ten Speed Press, 1996).

Using the Internet in Your Job Search by Fred E. Jandt and Mary Nemnich (Indianapolis, Ind.: 1995).

NETWORKING

The vast majority of jobs are found through the informal (i.e., unlisted) job market. That means you have to network. This book tells you how.

The Networking Book by Jeffrey Stamp and Jessica Lipnak (New York: Routledge & Kegan Paul, 1986).

THE NEW WORK WORLD

The following books describe how the work world has changed under the influence of a global economy and rapid technological changes. They all offer extremely helpful career management strategies designed to increase your independence from and buffer you against unpredictable corporate ups and downs.

The Age of Unreason by Charles Handy (Boston: Harvard Business School Press, 1989).

Creating You and Company: Learn to Think like the CEO of Your Own Career by William Bridges (Reading, Mass.: Addison-Wesley, 1997).

The New Rules: How to Succeed in Today's Post-Corporate World by John P. Kotter (New York: The Free Press, 1995).

JobShift: How to Prosper in a Workplace Without Jobs by William Bridges (Reading, Mass.: Addison-Wesley, 1994).

Job Shock: Four New Principles Transforming Our Work and Business by Harry S. Dent, Jr. (New York: St. Martin's, 1995).

We Are All Self-Employed: The New Social Contract for Working in a Changed World by Cliff Hakim (San Francisco: Berrett-Koehler, 1993).

The following book and article are written for employers rather than individuals, but for that reason they provide you with an inside look at how businesses think about workplace trends. David Noer's book includes a helpful summary of the shift in the implicit contract between employers and employees. Betsy Collard's article will help you understand what criteria to apply in seeking employers who provide support for "career resilience" (i.e., taking responsibility for your own career development, retirement planning, and keeping your skills up to date).

Healing the Wound: Overcoming the Trauma of Layoffs and Revitalizing Downsized Organizations by David Noer (San Francisco: Jossey-Bass, 1993).

"Toward a Career-Resilient Workforce" by Betsy Collard, R. Waterman, and J. Waterman (*Harvard Business Review,* July/August, 1994).

OVERCOMING BARRIERS TO SUCCESS

This book describes some of the most common pitfalls to achieving goals. It is extremely useful for anyone feeling stuck. Susan Schenkel explains how to diagnose your obstacles and design practical, straightforward strategies to move forward.

Giving Away Success: Why Women Get Stuck and What to Do About It by Susan Schenkel (New York: Random House, 1991).

Lois Frankel's book explains why some of the skills and attitudes that helped you succeed in one stage of your career may have to be stretched and altered to advance in today's work world. She emphasizes self-knowledge and interpersonal skills, and includes lots of exercises and practical suggestions for networking, teamwork, and "managing up."

Overcoming Your Strengths: 8 Reasons Why Successful People Derail and How to Get Back on Track by Lois Frankel (New York: Harmony, 1997).

RESOURCES FOR PARENTS

This book is invaluable for parents who want to help their children explore different career options. It suggests strategies, activities, and resources appropriate for children at different developmental stages, provides a useful summary of tests and interest inventories, and offers solid and clear information and advice.

Career Coaching Your Kids: Guiding Your Child Through the Process of Career Discovery by David Montross, Theresa Kane, and Robert Ginn (Palo Alto, Calif.: Davies-Black, 1997).

SURVIVORS OF ABUSE

This book celebrates the strength and resiliency of abuse survivors who have managed to heal, grow, and transcend their pain.

Strong at the Broken Places: Overcoming the Effects of Childhood Abuse by Linda Tschirhart Sanford (New York: Random House, 1990).

This popular guide has helped many women survivors of childhood sexual abuse find strategies for healing, confidence in themselves, and hope in their ability gradually to recover completely from the trauma of sexual abuse.

The Courage to Heal: A Guide for Women Survivors of Child Sexual Abuse by Ellen Bass and Laura Davis (New York: Harper and Row, 1988).

This guidebook is an invaluable resource for survivors of childhood abuse. It clearly explains how abuse can affect adults' expectations of work, their feelings of vulnerability at work, and challenges that may arise in relationships with colleagues. It describes situations likely to produce stress for survivors, and suggests effective coping strategies to manage stress. The authors suggest many tangible steps survivors can take to create safe and nurturing work environments, including a list of questions to use in assessing the health of different work climates. Especially useful is a list of job possibilities keyed to different stages of healing and recovery and a section outlining specific skills and strengths that people acquire through the process of overcoming trauma. The book is available from the authors: Career Resources Book Dept., 1051 Beacon St., #101, Brookline, MA 02446. Or phone (617) 732-1200.

Thriving at Work: A Guidebook for Survivors of Childhood Abuse by Nancy Brook and Cynthia Krainin (Brookline, Mass.: Career Resources, 1998).

This fascinating book describes the links among survivors of many kinds of violence and trauma, from war to childhood physical and sexual abuse. Informative, compassionate, and wise, it summarizes lots of research and includes clinical examples. It will expand your knowledge of the individual and social price of violence.

Trauma and Recovery by Judith Herman (New York: Basic Books, 1992).

THEORETICAL AND CLINICAL RESOURCES

These listings are for clinicians or others who want to learn more about Murray Bowen's intergenerational family systems theory. *The Atlantic Monthly* article provides an excellent summary of Bowen's work.

"Chronic Anxiety and Defining a Self: An Introduction to Murray Bowen's Theory of Human Emotional Functioning" by Michael Kerr (*Atlantic Monthly,* September 1988).

Family Therapy in Clinical Practice by Murray Bowen (New York: Jason Aronson, 1978).

Alice Miller's groundbreaking book offers a psychoanalytic perspective on parents' quest for healing through their children, focusing on "gifted children" who become psychotherapists.

The Drama of the Gifted Child: The Search for the True Self by Alice Miller (New York: Basic Books, 1994).

If you're interested in the concept of a "family unconscious," this book presents research and case examples to define and explore it.

The Family Unconscious by E. Bruce Taub-Bynum (Wheaton, Ill.: Quest Books, 1984).

This book tells you everything you need to know to prepare a genogram, or family tree, for your family. It also describes how clinicians can use genograms in working with families.

Genograms in Family Assessment by Monica McGoldrick (New York: Norton, 1985).

David Allen synthesizes Bowen's and other family systems theories with theories of individual psychological development, and presents a step-by-step description of his own style of integrated therapy.

Unifying Individual and Family Therapies by David Allen (San Francisco: Jossey-Bass, 1988).

JOURNAL WRITING FOR PERSONAL GROWTH

For anyone who likes to write, this book teaches you a journal-writing method you can use to explore the patterns and themes that link your work and personal lives together. Intensive journal entries enable you to create a synthetic dialogue between your inner and outer lives. If you enjoyed **Exercise 15-2,** "Dialogue with a Dead or Absent Relative," you will find in this book a format for similar dialogues you can write with People, Works, Events, or Society. This method is a powerful tool for personal growth and transformation and can help you understand where you've been, where you are now, and where you're headed. Intensive journal workshops are offered by trained facilitators throughout the United States. You can acquire information about workshops in your area from Dialogue House in New York. Call (212) 673-5880.

At a Journal Workshop: The Basic Text and Guide for Using the Intensive Journal by Ira Progroff (New York: Dialogue House, 1975).

VALUES AND BUSINESS

The following books adopt a philosophical stance toward contemporary corporate values and practices. They offer frameworks for exploring the links—and disconnections—between your personal and spiritual values and those of the workplace. They offer suggestions on ways to integrate ecological and humanistic values with the economic demands of the marketplace. They do not sugarcoat the problems and challenges of taming the corporate beast, but they are all optimistic and inspirational in tone and substance.

The Heart Aroused: Poetry and the Preservation of the Soul in Corporate America by David Whyte (New York: Currency Doubleday, 1994).
The Hungry Spirit: Beyond Capitalism, A Quest for Purpose in the Modern World by Charles Handy (New York: Broadway Books, 1998).
The Paradox of Success: When Winning at Work Means Losing at Life by John R. O'Neill (Los Angeles: Jeremy Tarcher, 1993).
Reinventing Work by Matthew Fox (San Francisco: HarperCollins, 1994).
The Stirring of Soul in the Workplace by Alan Briskin (San Francisco: Jossey-Bass, 1996).

Index

About the Author

Mary Jacobsen has more than fifteen years' experience as a teacher, counselor, career coach, and workshop leader. She maintains a psychotherapy practice in Arlington, Massachusetts, and offers lectures and workshops nationally on "Hand-Me-Down Dreams: How Families Influence Our Career Paths." She also offers workshops on leadership development, midlife and midcareer transitions, coping with change and loss, and coaching skills for supervisors and managers. She often uses storytelling and mythology to make her presentations accessible and engaging.

Jacobsen has coached hundreds of people through work and life transitions by helping them transform barriers to successful change into sources of learning, strength, and growth. She has lectured to numerous professional, community, adult, and continuing education groups, including the Eastern College and Employer Network, Harvard University's Office of Career Services, the Cambridge Center for Adult Education, the National Association of Social Workers, the International Women's Forum, the International Association of Career Management Professionals, Brandeis University, Bentley College, and the University of Texas at Austin. She has taught college courses at Wheelock College, Canisius College, and SUNY/Buffalo, and served as an assistant dean at Empire State College of the State University of New York.

Jacobsen received a B.A. in English from the College of William and Mary and a Ph.D. in English from the State University of New York at Buffalo. She received a master's degree in social work from Boston University's Graduate School of Social Work.